BANISH » BACK « P·A·I·N

Effective self-help with the aid of simple home remedies

ROGER NEWMAN TURNER
B.Ac., N.D., D.O., M.R.O.

Illustrations by Giles Newman Turner

THORSONS PUBLISHING GROUP

First published 1989

For the special people

© Roger Newman Turner 1989

British Library Cataloguing in Publication Data
Newman Turner, Roger, *1940*–
  Banish back pain.
  1. Man. Back. Backache. Relief of alternative methods
  I. Title
  616.7'306

ISBN 0-7225-1849-8

Published by Thorsons Publishers Limited,
Wellingborough, Northamptonshire, NN8 2RQ,
England.

Printed in Great Britain by Mackays of Chatham, Kent

10 9 8 7 6 5 4 3 2

Contents

Acknowledgements

Years of knowledge and experience go into the development of an integrated approach to back pain; not just personal experience, but that of colleagues who contributed insights and expertise which have been digested slowly over the decades to feed my own particular procedures. Way back, Keith Lamont, Tom Dummer, Alfred Manley, and the late Parnell Bradbury gave precision and new directions to my understanding of the back. More recently, Fritz Frederick Smith has supplemented subtler nuances with the gentle power of his Zero Balancing system.

During the preparation of this manual, my colleagues, Martin L. Budd and Peter M. Goldman, have contributed valuable information, while Bonnie Moonayer, of The Back Shop, was helpful with a survey of the latest equipment. The tedious task of transcribing this manuscript to disk was carried through with speed and efficiency by Lynne Metcalfe. The illustrations were done by my brother, Giles Newman Turner.

I am grateful to all these for their wisdom and skills, but also to my patients for the challenges they have brought me. They have taught me much, and I go on learning.

Introduction

The first and most important thing to be said about back pain is that you don't have to put up with it. This is a book of practical advice, and the first advice, if you are suffering pain or discomfort, is to turn to Chapter 14 where you will find a number of measures you can put into practice right away to gain some positive relief.

All too often people with back pain are fobbed off with some pain-killers and just told to rest, because 'there is nothing you can do about it!' Certainly rest is valuable, but back pain is not simply a problem which afflicts you without reason and over which you have no control. There are many resources in your home that may be used to relieve your pain and help you to cope more effectively — simple physical procedures which can alleviate the discomfort whilst helping the healing process, and strategies for improving the back using the most up-to-date nutritional knowledge.

The way in which you use your back, in the home, at work or at play, can exert a considerable influence on the pattern of pain. Correct use of the back is important and we shall look at ways of using it with maximum effect and minimum effort, but this is not just another book of exercises and 'how to lift' drawings. We shall also explore the other vital ingredients of a healthy back and I shall explain how you can contribute to its maintenance to make it more manageable and conducive to comfortable function.

More than mechanical

A sense of helplessness, coupled with ignorance, is often cultivated by the belief that back pain is a purely mechanical problem beyond our personal control. Displaced bones, 'trapped nerves', arthritic joints, and spastic muscles are all blamed for the pains as if they were unavoidable afflictions.

Back health, however, is a question not just of mechanics but of dynamics — the way in which the different parts of the spine move in relation to each other, the balance of the tensions in muscles and ligaments, their tone and elasticity, and the quality of the very important packing material which lies between them, the collagen tissues.

Of course, some back problems can be devastatingly debilitating, defying the most exhaustive efforts to ease them, and I do not suggest that this book will provide all the answers. Quite often, however, a better response is achieved by combining resources and paying attention to the several aspects of the disorder. For example, if you are already having treatment of some sort, it will be more beneficial if you can improve the health of the back as well. You will find in this book many measures which you can use to complement and get more out of whatever professional help you obtain, be it osteopathy, chiropractic, acupuncture, or orthopaedic surgery.

Supporting treatment

An osteopathic adjustment or an operation, no matter how skilful, will not be the end of your back disorder. You will still need constructive advice on rehabilitation and correct use to minimize further trouble. If you have not already sought professional treatment we shall also take a look at the options available so that you can be guided towards what is appropriate to your particular problem.

Most treatment is directed at one level of the problem, usually the mechanical level, or the relief of pain, but the overall health of the back has to be your personal responsibility. Experience has shown that response to treatment is better where people also work on improving the health of the back as a whole, using the methods recommended in this book.

Back pain is one of the biggest disruptors of personal and professional life. In the United Kingdom alone, 33 million work days per year are lost through back troubles and this costs the taxpayer approaching £200 million in sickness benefits. This does not account for the millions of sufferers who soldier on in discomfort. Add the cost of surgery and other special treatments, and the price of back pain becomes quite staggering. These depressing figures could be significantly reduced, and the discomfort of millions greatly alleviated, if more use were made of some simple common sense procedures with the resources to be found in every home.

Understanding the problem is half the battle of solving it and I hope that, by working through these pages, you will be equipped with a means of taking some positive steps towards banishing your back pain.

1. BUILT FOR ACTION

The anatomy of the back

In an ideal world none of us would be aware of our backs and necks; we would know them only as a part of the freely flowing, wonderfully working unit that is our body. Like a leopard we should glide through daily life, leaping to the needs of the moment without a thought of anything but the task in hand.

The regrettable reality is all too evident to many people. For most, experience of the back is an unpleasant one: stiffness and reluctance to respond to the need for movement on waking in the morning; creaking and crackles in the neck through the day; and annoying aches and weariness as the day draws in. Added to this, for some people, may be the surprise of a seizure which can immobilize the whole body with alarming suddenness.

The most frightening thing about neck and back pain is not knowing quite what is going on. If you are not familiar with the structures involved, you are liable to imagine all sorts of problems; it's a bit like being lost in strange countryside without a map to guide you. Besides that, the spine and its anatomical associates, such as muscles and ligaments, can be a mischievous mimic of other disorders, for example in the head or chest, where it can conjure up pains suggestive of a tumour or a heart attack when no such thing is present.

Before we look at why backache bothers us it will be worth considering what is involved — we need to study the map in order to become familiar with the territory. This will help us understand the nature of back pain and, above all, how to alleviate it more effectively.

A remarkable design

If we are to consider all the anatomical structures involved in backache, we need to think about the whole skeletal system from the skull right down to the feet. An imbalance of bones at either end of the body can initiate a backache, as we shall see later. For the moment, though, we must concentrate on the spine itself, or rather, the whole back, because it is not just the bones that give the trouble.

When we consider the variety of functions which it has to perform, the spinal column really is a remarkable piece of engineering. Were it newly created, it would undoubtedly win a few design awards — though, like all new innovations, its imperfections might still draw criticism!

Fig 1 The spinal column is supported by muscles which are like the guy ropes on a radio mast

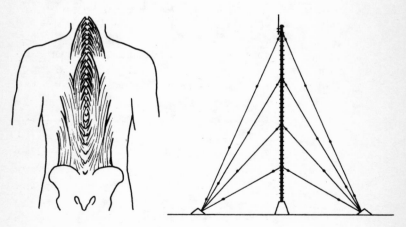

Our backs are designed for:

Stability — the spine and its ligaments act as the main supporting column of the body. The structure of the bones gives anchorage to the muscles and ligaments, enabling them to act like the guy-ropes on a tent or radio mast (Fig 1).

Mobility — we need to be able to walk, run, bend, and turn, which would not be possible if the spine were one solid rod; so it consists of a number of bones which are able to move in various directions and collectively give us flexibility without loss of stability. The size and structure of the bones in the spinal column vary from top to bottom so that we have a wide range of movement in the neck and more solid support in the lower back. The bones also have projections to which the muscles are attached to give leverage for our movements.

Protection — the bones in the spinal column are also designed to give a protective armour to the nerve cord which extends down from the base of the brain. Nerves from this cord pass out between each pair of bones to supply the skin, muscles, and internal organs. In the chest area the bones of the spine also have attachments for the ribs which protect the vital organs in the chest such as the lungs and heart.

The flexible framework

However much we may change on the surface, even within our own lifetime, our basic structure has not altered greatly in many thousands of years. Next time you go to a museum, take a little time to study the skeleton of one of our primitive ancestors. They were a little smaller, perhaps, but their bones were the same as ours.

Notice the spine in particular. You will see a column of small spiky structures, wider and thicker at the bottom, becoming finer and thinner at the top. These are the vertebrae (Fig 2). Each one consists of a solid cylindrical part at the front, for support, and a ring of bone with attachments for muscles and ligaments at the back. In life the rings protect the spinal cord and nerves which extend from the base of the brain, while between the solid vertebral bodies are fibrous flexible discs, rather like spongy washers which permit movement between the individual bones of the column.

The health of our backs is not just a matter of the bones and discs. Binding them together are ligaments and muscles of varying length and strength which enable them to move or maintain a reasonable alignment. In addition there are nerves which motivate the muscles and vessels which carry the blood to nourish them and clear away the waste products they produce when working.

Fig 2 The spinal column (viewed from the left side)

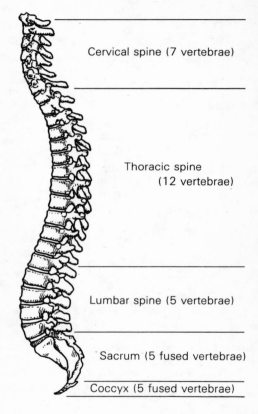

Cervical spine (7 vertebrae)

Thoracic spine
(12 vertebrae)

Lumbar spine (5 vertebrae)

Sacrum (5 fused vertebrae)

Coccyx (5 fused vertebrae)

Perhaps the most important yet most neglected part of our back's anatomy is the 'packing material' which lies between all these structures — the connective tissue. This provides the elasticity and acts as the forwarding agent between the blood vessels and other structures of the spine. It helps to support the muscles and ligaments and protects the blood vessels and bones. It maintains the flexibility as well as providing stability to our spines, and in addition acts as an insulator against the changes of temperature and moisture in the atmosphere which, we shall see, can affect the overall comfort of our backs.

Fig 3 Vertebrae, while basically similar in structure, vary in size and shape to meet the demands at different levels of the spinal column

CERVICAL VERTEBRA (× ½)
(viewed from behind and above)

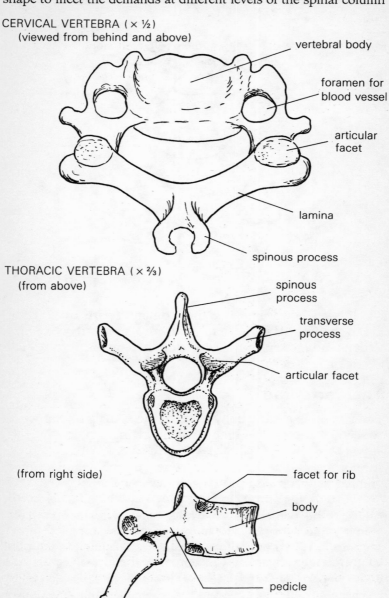

vertebral body

foramen for blood vessel

articular facet

lamina

spinous process

THORACIC VERTEBRA (× ⅔)
(from above)

spinous process

transverse process

articular facet

(from right side)

facet for rib

body

pedicle

LUMBAR VERTEBRA (× ½)
(from above)

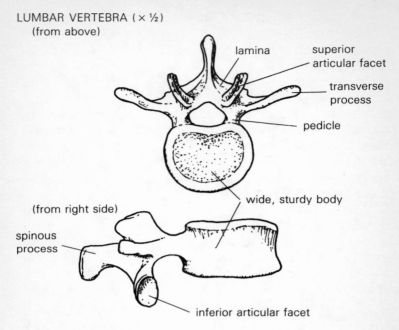

Let us see how well suited these different parts of our backs are to the tasks they have to perform. Perhaps then we shall understand more clearly how we often allow them to fall into disrepair and develop backache.

The vertebrae

The vertebrae are the bony units of the spinal column which collectively permit it to move whilst giving protection to the spinal cord and nerves. Each vertebra consists of a cylindrical supporting part at the front known as the body and a ring of bone at the back with protruberances to provide attachments for the muscles and ligaments. (See Fig 3.) The sides of the ring are the pedicles from which facets extend above and below to meet those of the neighbouring vertebrae. The arch is completed by the laminae meeting at the back to form the spinous process, the tips of which you can feel as you run your fingers down the spine. In thinner people it is also possible to feel the transverse processes which protrude from the sides of the pedicles. They are about an inch (2 cm) out on either side from the spinous processes.

The proportions and thickness of these parts of the vertebrae vary according to the degree of movements needed at different levels of the spinal column. In the lower back, for instance, firmness, strength, and support are provided by large vertebral bodies and sturdy pedicles to give attachments for the strong lumbar muscles. Further up the spine, in the thoracic region, from the waist up to the shoulders the vertebrae become progressively smaller with narrower bodies. They have less weight to bear and finer muscles to move them but they are capable of a greater range of movement and also provide an attachment for the ribs which protect our heart and lungs.

In the neck even more flexibility is needed and the vertebrae are quite thin, but strong enough to support the head and protect the spinal cord, which at this level gives rise to many important nerves.

Discs

Separating each vertebra is a fibrous plate known as the intervertebral disc. The outer parts of the disc are quite tough but, like some sweets, it has a softer centre. This gives it flexibility so that a small degree of movement is possible between each pair of bones. (See Fig 4.)

Fig 4 Cross-section of a disc

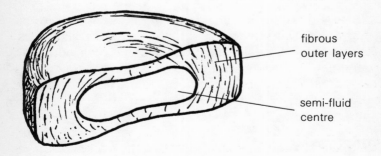

fibrous
outer layers

semi-fluid
centre

Quite a wide range of movement is possible in the spine when a group of vertebrae move together. In fact there is no solitary action by a joint; every movement involves several vertebrae in an area.

The disc also acts as a buffer between the bones as we stand, walk, or run. The constant changes of pressure in the discs as we go about our daily activities alters the amount of fluid and sponginess in them. The combined effect through the whole spine can be quite significant in a heavily built person, who may lose up to half an inch (1 cm) in height during the course of the day. At night when we are at rest, with no pressure on the back, our discs can reabsorb fluid and, with it, nourishment.

The spinal shock absorbers

The intervertebral discs are designed to act as shock absorbers in the spinal column; without them every step we take would be a real bone-shaker!

Each disc is like a thick, porous rubber, consisting of fibrous material and about 85 per cent water. The outer parts of the disc are more fibrous while the fluid concentrates towards the centre. The upper and lower surface of the disc is a cartilaginous layer called an end plate, and this acts as a sieve between the disc and the bone. Discs have no blood supply so they depend on a process of diffusion through the end plates. Regular movement is essential to encourage this diffusion.

When we are resting or sleeping, the disc sucks in water and nutrients. When we are on the move, compression squeezes the fluids out and expels waste products, such as lactic acid. Most of us lose about a centimetre in height during the day and regain it again at night.

Muscles

It is our muscles which enable us to move. They also play an important part in keeping the vertebrae in proper balance.

Each muscle consists of thousands of spindle-shaped fibres which contract and relax according to the messages the brain

The 'slipped disc'

Contrary to popular misconception, discs cannot slip. The term 'slipped disc' is often wrongly used to describe injuries which are due to a variety of other causes, most commonly a misalignment of the vertebrae. The discs are held firmly in place by strong ligaments so have little scope for individual movement, but they can become quite severely compressed in heavily built individuals.

Occasionally a disc may rupture when subjected to a sudden severe compression. This is called a disc herniation. The soft centre is squeezed out through the fibrous casing and may cause pressure on the nerve cord or nerves passing from it. The pain is usually very intense and incapacitating. Fortunately, disc herniation is comparatively rare as a cause of back pain; even quite severe episodes of back pain are likely to be due to other structures being out of balance with each other and will usually be alleviated by the measures described in this book or the attentions of a skilled professional, such as an osteopath or chiropractor.

sends them through the nerves. (See Fig 5.) Every muscle fibre should work in harmony with its fellows but sometimes small groups remain contracted after working and form fibrous nodules or larger areas of spasm. This working part of the muscle is attached to the bone by a tougher material, the tendon. Tendons are less elastic than muscles and have a poorer blood supply. They are, therefore, slower to recover from injury.

Ligaments

Ligaments, too, have a poor blood supply. They also need to be firm and secure since they must hold the joints together, allowing them to move through their normal range but without too much play. They provide stability, like guy ropes, but have to be sufficiently flexible to permit reasonable mobility. (See Fig 6.)

Fig 5 Muscle and tendons, showing magnification of skeletal muscle
fibres (striated muscle)

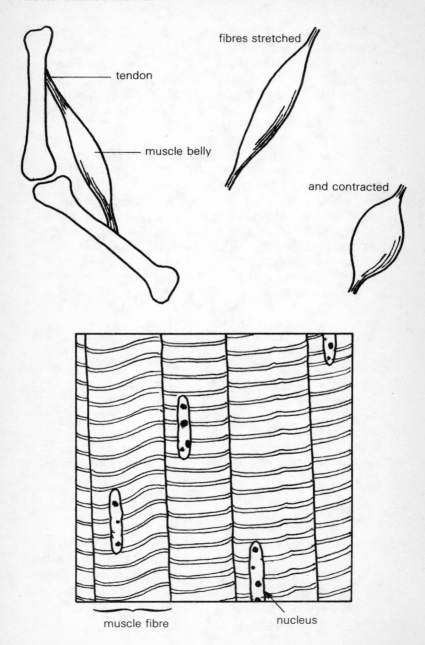

Fig 6 The anterior ligament of the spine helps to stabilize the vertebrae and the discs

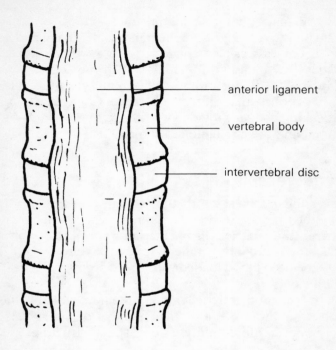

anterior ligament

vertebral body

intervertebral disc

   Ligaments can be overstretched and too slack or they can thicken up and become fibrous if they do not have the right degree of help from the muscles in keeping the joints balanced. While many people associate back pain with stiffness and restriction of the joints, it is commonly the consequence of poor ligament tone and hypermobile joints which do not stay in the correct position.

Connective tissue

Filling the space between the bones, tendons, muscles, and ligaments is a versatile and vital material, the connective tissue or collagen. Connective tissue takes a number of different forms, as it makes cartilage, vessels, or fatty tissue. Its chief function in the back is that of supporting and binding, helping to maintain the resilience and strength. It forms the fibres which bind the tendons to bones and buffers the muscles and ligaments as they move alongside each other.

Connective tissue is more than just packing material. It plays an important role in the transport of nutrients and waste products to and from the muscles, tendons, and bones. If it becomes weak or congested there will be inadequate elasticity, or pain and inflammation in the spine.

Much of the filling and protective connective tissue is composed of collagen, a protein substance. Collagen can only be made if the body is provided with the right raw materials from its food and the circulation is sufficiently effective to carry it to the tissues.

Blood vessels

Traversing each side of the spinal column, giving off numerous branches, are the arteries, which wind their way between the muscles, ligaments, and bones to supply them with blood and nourishment, and the veins, which carry away the used blood loaded with waste products of the back's activities.

Both the blood and the lymph — the fluid which bathes the connective tissues — are efficient ways of transporting the energy needed for healthy, strong spinal structures.

Nerves

If it were not for the nerves, back pain might not be such a problem, but we would be in a pretty useless state without them. Nerves transmit messages from the brain and spinal cord to the rest of the body, initiating the movement of a muscle or secretion of a gland and also the information from the body to the brain, such as the sensation of the fur when we stroke our cat or a pain in a spastic muscle.

The spinal cord extends from the base of the brain down to the level of the lower thoracic vertebrae. Between each bone of the spinal column it sends out a nerve root on each side which divides into two branches. The front branch supplies the internal organs, such as the lungs or kidneys, while the back branches become the communication with the skin and muscles on the surface of the body.

Nerves which emerge from the lower part of the back hang

down from the base of the cord like a horse's tail inside the spinal column. Hence they are known as the *cauda equina*. The roots emerging from the lumbar area are particularly thick and several join together again to form the sciatic nerve which supplies the legs and feet.

Although nerves primarily transmit pain or other impulses from the body to the spinal cord and brain they may also send pain messages out to the surface if they are irritated by pressure near their origin in the spine. Many pains of the arms and legs or of the rib cage may originate in the neck and back. Pressure around the roots of the nerves may also have a negative effect on the organs which they supply. If there is impairment of the impulses in the nerves supplying the stomach or liver, for example, those organs may gradually become less efficient at performing their functions of digestion and absorption.

This link from body surface to internal organs is known as the *somatico-visceral reflex*. It can work both ways so that pain from, say, the gall bladder may be felt in the back or shoulders.

The harmony of the back

All the parts of the back are designed to work in harmony, to keep us moving freely and comfortably but, as many thousands of people are painfully aware, it does not always act so smoothly. Could this be a clue to a flaw in the basic design of our backs or to other factors?

Let us see why back pain occurs.

2. CAUSE AND EFFECT

The reasons for backache

The only real awareness many people have of their back is a painful one. Perception of pain varies enormously but, whatever your threshold, it spells discomfort of some sort which can invariably be relieved.

Here are some of the descriptions of pain or unpleasant sensations which patients have described to me in recent weeks:

* headaches with pressure behind the eyes
* headaches with a tight band around the skull
* a sharp pain every time I turn my head to one side
* a burning pain in the shoulders radiating to the back of the head
* agonizing pain in the ribs every time I cough
* a feeling of constriction in the chest; unable to take a deep breath
* numbness or tingling in the hand or arm
* stiffness of the middle back or waist
* acute pain across the lower back
* sharp pain on one side of the back radiating to the buttock and thigh
* a tingling and numbness of the legs and feet
* I feel as if I don't fit together properly.

There are many more similar tales. Perhaps you recognize one of these or could add others. They are all symptoms which involve the neck and back or which originate there. If we add the variety of other disorders which can be aggravated by back problems — such as digestive troubles, chest diseases, and poor eyesight — you can appreciate how very important the spine is.

But why do we get these pains? One medical expert has stated that 70 per cent of back pain is idiopathic (without known cause) but if you think about the structure of the spine, described in the last chapter, and consider the ways we can use and abuse it, then it is not too difficult to find a variety of explanations for the difficulties which afflict back sufferers. Armed with this knowledge it is then possible to develop ways of improving the situation and relieving the pain.

The onset of back pain

Back pain doesn't just happen in an instant. The causes of the disorders develop gradually over many months or even years. There is usually a long prelude of postural abuse, inadequate exercise, insufficient nourishment, and neglect of early-warning signs.

The tying of the shoe-lace or reaching up for the storage jar are only the final insult — the point at which the back is no longer able to sustain its normal functions after a long period of progressive deterioration.

Comparatively minor everyday movements can suddenly become a major undertaking when the back seizes up, but it rarely does this without there having been a long spell of stiffness or twinges when first getting going in the morning, or impaired movement after sitting in a chair for a while in the evening.

Brief moments of inconvenience, if neglected, may eventually become time-consuming days of incapacity. Unfortunately, it is not always possible to recognize the warning signs and as we vary so much in the mechanical efficiency of our bodies, what starts as a vague ache may become a major impairment for some and remain a mild annoyance for others.

The unlucky ones may be quite fit in most respects — often

physically active people — but their particular posture or the dynamics of their muscles and ligaments make them vulnerable to back pain. There is a wide range of reasons why backs and necks can become such a problem.

Causes of pain

The actual causes of pain can be narrowed down to mechanical and chemical factors.

Mechanical causes arise from the structure of the muscles, ligaments, and bones themselves. They may include abnormal postural stresses, direct compression from bones which have become too close together, swellings due to injury or acute inflammation, and distention of veins in the area of the spinal nerves.

Chemical irritants can be associated with inflammation; they are produced by the tissues as a means of defence. Much more rarely other substances, such as the dyes injected into the spinal canal for certain X-ray investigations, may cause irritation. The chemical irritants stimulate pain-registering nerves, causing contraction of related muscles which in turn produce waste products that act as further irritants and so perpetuate the spasm.

Quite often a *muscular pain* might become superimposed on a pain which is basically mechanical. In other words the discomfort from spasm in muscles may add to or take over from that which is caused by the joint displacements.

Another cause of pain in the back may be through *reflex irritation* from internal organs. Nerves from organs such as the gall bladder, when it is inflamed or in spasm, may convey impulses to the spinal cord which then sends messages out along the surface nerve of the same segment causing pain in the muscles around the shoulder blade.

Most of these causes of back pain can be successfully treated, but to get a better idea of what is needed we should look at them in a little more detail.

Bone displacements

The notion of the 'slipped disc' is one of the most common myths in medicine. People talk of the slipped disc as the cause of their back pain and the misconception is even fuelled by some loose-talking doctors and osteopaths! But, as explained in Chapter 1, there is no such thing.

What is really meant by people who use the term 'slipped disc' too loosely is possibly a displacement of the vertebrae or 'a bone out of place'. Even this is a somewhat misleading term; there can be misalignment of vertebrae in relation to each other but it is unusual for bones individually to make any major change of position (see Fig 7). They may become fixed in a part of their normal range of movement so they do not return to the balanced resting position.

So, when you visit an osteopath or chiropractor and you hear the clicking sound as an adjustment is made, this is not 'putting the bone back' but releasing a fixation of the joints.

The position or mobility of the bones in the back is critically important to your everyday comfort but this does not mean that you have to have the perfect S-curve in order to keep well. There are plenty of people who can function efficiently and freely with many variations on the basic pattern which we have evolved. Nevertheless, the sort of positions you habitually adopt at work, rest, or play can put a considerable strain on certain parts of the spine and cause some problems.

Posture

The way we stand, sit, or use our bodies has a considerable influence on the efficiency of our backs. Lazy postural habits may start at an early age. Slouching in front of the TV may not cause too much harm for a young flexible spine but, continued through the teens and twenties it can gradually create changes of natural spinal alignment which lay the foundations for wear in the joints, abnormal muscle contractions, and tensions through the thirties, forties, and fifties. Areas of restricted mobility or alterations of the normal curves cause stress points which may lead to locking of individual vertebrae or painful spasm of surrounding muscle fibres.

The same sort of problems may arise from excessive one-sided use in your work or pastimes. The typist who has to

Fig 7 When one brick shifts, others in the column must move to prevent it from toppling...

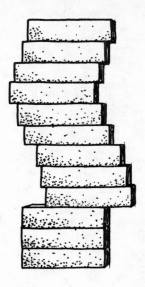

...when one vertebra is misaligned, others must move to compensate

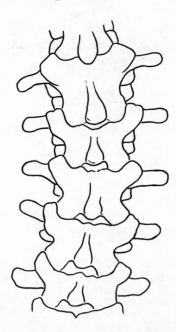

copy from documents to one side of the typewriter may, eventually, develop tension in the neck and shoulders which can lead to vertebral misalignments in the neck or upper back, with a progressively restricted range of movement. Some sports, such as golf or tennis, involve a degree of one-sidedness which may contribute to the positional stresses at certain points in the spine.

This does not mean you will have to give up these activities permanently if you develop back pain, but it is sensible to become aware of the ways in which you use your body. Postural awareness is an important part of good back care and, together with other steps to maintain health, can enable you to go on enjoying sports and benefiting from the exercise they provide.

Each person's problems may be unique but there are some basic rules about using our bodies which can minimize the stresses and strains of our everyday activities. There are also valuable systems, such as the Alexander technique, which help you to develop postural awareness. We shall look at these, and much more, later in this book.

Some indirect causes of backache

At times the back will hurt because of disorders elsewhere in the body rather than problems with the spinal structures themselves. It is important to recognize when your backache is caused by more than the muscles and joints. Most pains in the muscles and joints can be distinguished by the fact that they are usually aggravated or ameliorated by a change of position.

If you think any of the following conditions may be causing your back pain you should consult your doctor, naturopath, or osteopath.

Fevers and influenza may cause general muscular aches, especially in the middle of the back. These will go as the crisis resolves with a cold or diarrhoea.

Some indirect causes of backache

Pleurisy is an inflammation of the pleural membrane, or outer lining of the lungs. Pain is often referred to the chest wall on one or both sides and may be aggravated by breathing deeply or coughing. The condition is often accompanied by fever and a short dry cough in the acute stage.

Kidney disease may cause deep pain in the lower thoracic or lumbar area. It is usually located around the back of the lower ribs and, unlike low back pain, will usually be present whatever position you adopt.

Gynaecological disorders such as prolapse, uterine displacement, fibroids, and premenstrual congestion may cause pain in the lower back. The pain is usually central and is not affected by position. It is mostly caused by the reflex stretching of the uterine ligaments.

Constipation is sometimes responsible for discomfort across the lower back.

Osteoporosis, which is due to loss of calcium from the bones of the spine, especially in women after the menopause, causes backache. The weakened spinal bones start to curve, putting extra strain on the muscles.

Firm foundations

Our feet are our foundations. They carry us through life hardly entering our consciousness until something goes wrong. A splinter in the heel or an ill-fitting pair of shoes can soon make us painfully aware of their importance.

Have you thought about the effect on your back when you start to limp? There are immediate changes in the dynamics of the muscles and ligaments and, if the foot problem persists, there may soon be some stiffening and alterations in the alignment of the vertebrae to accommodate your lopsided walk.

Scoliosis

A sideways curve of the spine, which should appear straight when viewed from behind, is known as a scoliosis, and the condition seems to be on the increase in children and adolescents. There is usually a primary curve to one side and a secondary one in the opposite direction above or below it.

Slight scoliosis is common in many people with vertebral displacements which temporarily alter the alignment of the spinal column, but the causes of the more pronounced curvature of growing children are not clearly established. Theories suggested include seating and standing babies upright at too early an age in infant car-seats and push-chairs, unequal muscular development on one side owing to the dominance of one leg during the important crawling stage of development, and bad postural habits later in the teens creating vertebral displacements.

Treatments include the use of body braces, electrical stimulation of muscles, and surgery. A gentler and more promising initial approach should be an opinion from an osteopath or chiropractor.

So get those shoes stretched, see a chiropodist about those corns or callouses, and make sure that that blister is healing satisfactorily if you want to keep your back out of trouble.

Muscle spasms

Muscles and ligaments are like guy ropes supporting the spinal column, helping us to maintain the upright posture, and regulating the range of our activities. Guy ropes can become twisted, altering their pull on the structure they support, and muscles may do something similar.

They may contract in the normal way as we perform a movement but a number of fibres in the belly of the muscle may not return to full relaxation. This causes spasm which gives the muscle a nodular gritty feel when you touch it

The upright posture

There are some authorities who express the view that back pain is the result of a basic design fault. *Homo sapiens* pays the price of the upright posture in greater vulnerability to pressure and degeneration of the lower back joints. Certainly, a heavily built person imposes greater strain on the lower back joints and the vertical alignment of the spine makes it more sensitive to quite minor changes of position of the vertebrae.

Even a subtle shift of some of the bones in the pivotal areas of the spinal column, if they become fixed, can cause additional stress on other parts. Surrounding muscles and ligaments become either contracted or overstretched and in order to maintain the balance of the column the joints lower down may have to take extra strain. All this would be very different if we had a horizontal position like tigers, or horses, or dogs.

But isn't it likely that, in the hundreds of thousands of years since they adopted it, humans would have got used to the upright position? The spinal joints and muscles and ligaments have all had ample opportunity to adapt to the demands of walking tall. It is the loss of this capacity to adapt and maintain balance, tone, and elasticity, that causes back trouble, not the upright posture as such.

through the skin, instead of the smooth pliable sensation of relaxed fibres.

When the muscle fibres work they derive their energy from glycogen, the fuel derived from our food, and produce lactic acid as a waste product. If they do not return to the resting position of full relaxation they go on producing lactic acid, which acts as a further irritant to surrounding fibres so the area of stiffness may spread. The spasm of muscle fibres affects us in two ways. It limits our movements by preventing free mobility of the joints, and contracted fibres act as a source of irritation and pain.

Muscle contraction may eventually contribute to the locking of individual or specific groups of joints in the spinal column. The gradual spasm induced by repetitive tension in the muscles of the upper back between the shoulders, for example, eventually results in a restricted range of movement in the vertebrae of that area. It will also limit the free movement of the rib-cage which may impair the ease with which we breathe.

Muscle tensions of this type are probably a more common cause of back pain than the restricted joints or 'displaced bones' that are frequently blamed for the pain. Osteopathic or chiropractic correction of a restricted joint, or group of joints, can effect a remarkable and often rapid relief of an acute back pain but, without proper attention to the dynamics of the muscles and ligaments which support and stabilize the bones, the problem soon returns. There is very much more to a healthy back than well-adjusted joints.

Trigger points

The second significant contribution that muscles make to back problems is as sources of irritation and pain, not just in their immediate vicinity but in more distant areas. The contracted fibres of a muscle in spasm send impulses along the nerve to the spinal cord, in which they may move up or down several segments to set off a stream of impulses along a nerve leading to some other muscle or even organs within the body. The original spastic muscle is known as a 'trigger point' or focus of irritation. In fact, the sensation of pain or discomfort may be greater at the target site than at the guilty muscle itself. Quite often such trigger points may be 'silent' for most of the time, becoming evident only when they are sought by the skilled hands of an osteopath or experienced masseur or, perhaps, when we become extra tired or tense.

Most people have areas of contracted stiff muscles in their back or neck without being conscious of them. They develop gradually through faulty posture, repetitive movements, or continual anger, anxiety, or resentment. These trigger points may never cause any actual pain to some people yet can be a source of considerable discomfort to others. It all depends on individual pain thresholds or whether the muscle spasms have led to locking of the bones which may make them very much more sensitive.

The change in the angles of the vertebrae or, more usually, a group of vertebrae immediately affects the muscles that are attached to them. On one side — the side to which the bones tilt — the muscles will contract. If they were already in some spasm this will increase, perhaps sufficiently to cause pain or discomfort. The muscles on the outer side of the spinal curve created by the misalignment will be stretched. This happens during normal movement, after which the muscles return to their resting position, but if they remain stretched for long periods they will weaken.

The contracted muscles will be more painful at first and will, in any case, have to work harder to limit the movement of any joint which is causing irritation of a nerve.

Somatico-visceral reflex

What may seem a rather unfair consequence of contracted muscle fibres may be disturbances of function in deeper organs. Irritation from trigger points or pressure arising from misaligned vertebrae will track along the surface nerves to the spinal cord and then travel from these by deeper nerve fibres to organs such as the heart, lung, stomach, or intestines.

Fig 8 The somatico-visceral reflex

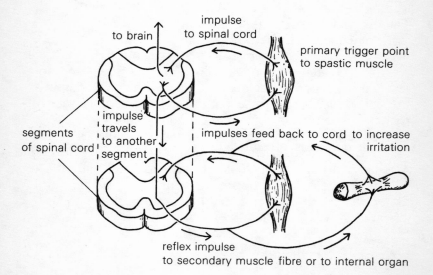

Chronic overstimulation of nerve fibres in the thoracic spine area, for example, may contribute to digestive disturbances. This is called a somatico-visceral reflex from *soma*, meaning body and *viscus*, meaning internal organ. (See Fig 8.)

It is also possible for the reflex to work the other way, the *viscero-somatic* reflex, dysfunction of the internal organ creating impulses which travel to the surface via the spinal cord. The best known example of this is the pain around the right shoulder and upper back owing to gall-bladder disease.

Stress and anxiety

'Does worry have anything to do with my back pain?' I am often asked. It certainly does. It may not be the cause of back trouble but it will aggravate any pains which are the result of the physical factors I have described.

If you have an old back injury or a chronic disorder you may find that it starts playing up when you are going through a stressful period. If it does not happen at the time it may well do so afterwards, just when you feel you can let go.

The link between your life situation and your stiff back may not be immediately obvious to you. There may be conflicts and frustrations simmering away at work or in your home to which you have long since become immune. But have you?

What about that stiff neck and shoulders which won't go away in spite of the osteopathy, massage, and exercise you have subjected them to? Why, do you suppose, are those low back muscles so tight and uncooperative when you want to get moving in the morning of every working day?

It is because your body is being more honest than your mind. Your mind may have adjusted to the unhappy situation by pushing it aside, rationalizing, and getting on with the immediate demands of daily life. Your body is governed by more primitive instincts: it wants to fight or run away and it prepares the muscles to do just that. It is motivated by the subconscious mind which never forgets that a problem still exists, that is until it can be satisfied that you have resolved it once and for all.

Until you do, the neck or back will probably go on seizing up every time the conflicts and tensions rear up. There are ways out of this trap and ways of coping better. Sometimes the ability to resolve a mental conflict is activated through release of the deeper physical tensions. If you want to be rid of your aches and pains you may need to confront these issues and you will find ways of doing this in Chapter 10: practical methods of relaxation and visualization which can help you to let go of some of the unnecessary burdens you may be carrying through life.

Weather prophets

Are you a weather prophet? Do you begin to ache whenever there is rain approaching? Perhaps you start to stiffen up in the cold windy weather. Many people with chronic joint problems, including neck and backache, are sensitive to changes in temperature and atmospheric pressure. They are able to predict the onset of a wet spell and have difficulty getting about in the winter.

Does climate really cause backache? Strictly speaking, no; no more than walking or driving a car, but if you already have a back which is vulnerable for any of the reasons described in this chapter then unsuitable weather conditions may aggravate your symptoms.

It is understandable that cold conditions will impair the circulation which could make stiffness more likely, but what about the onset of the wet weather? There appears to be no satisfactory explanation until we look at the physiology of Chinese medicine.

Traditional Chinese medicine, which embraces acupuncture, herbalism, manipulation, and dietary therapy, was evolved over a long period of time several thousand years ago. The principles established then and refined over the years explain the body's functions in terms of the movement of energies which are influenced by the changes of season. The basic energy of life, called *Chi*, has positive and negative qualities, *yang* and *yin*. Yang energy represents warmth, dryness, contraction, strength and surface protection, and when over-abundant is felt in the body as inflammation, congestion, and spasm. Yin energy regulates moisture, coolness, functions of the internal organs and, when allowed to dominate through lack of yang, is felt and seen as coldness, swellings, dull aches, and weakness.

If body defence is weak and there are chronic aches and pains, yin weather — damp and cold — superimposes on the already yin condition in the body and aggravates the symptoms. When defensive yang energy is deficient, the surface tissue also becomes vulnerable to invasion by what the ancient Chinese called 'external devils' — wind, cold, and damp. If you are digging in the garden on a windy day your efforts may make you perspire but the chilling effects of the wind may get in through the open pores and create stiffness. You may need an Epsom salts or mustard bath to sweat it out again but the acupuncture procedures of needling and warming with moxa herb are highly effective forms of relief.

Before you blame the weather entirely for your backache, remember that it is not the cause; it merely aggravates the symptoms. The real cause is within your body, the way it keeps a healthy balance of bones and muscles and, above all, the way it nourishes the supportive and protective tissues — in other words, the quality of the Chi.

Nutrition

You might find it difficult to make a connection between the food you eat and your back pain but the link is there, although an indirect one. I don't mean specific foods triggering off pains, like some sort of allergy or sensitivity (though in a few cases this may account for muscular pains), but the insidious process of poor nourishment and deficiency which creeps up on so many people through modern dietary habits.

Most people know about vitamins and minerals and think, particularly, of calcium because of its importance in preventing osteoporosis — the erosion of bone structure which occurs in middle age and beyond. But there are many other important nutrients which regulate the functions of back tissues.

Muscles, nerves, connective tissues, and bones all have special needs. They require adequate magnesium, potassium, vitamin C, and calcium. If they don't get them because our food is deficient, or our absorption of them is impaired by too much alcohol or smoking, then, sooner or later, those vital tissues start to fail in their task of supporting and moving the back effectively.

Yes, food and drink and the way we use them are important to healthy backs — so important that I have devoted a whole chapter to them. A positive approach to nutrition and the use of supplements, where necessary, is one of the major ways in which you can help to overcome your back pains.

Arthritis

The word arthritis is feared by most back pain sufferers. It is a fear without real foundation. The most common type of arthritis which affects the back is *osteo-arthritis*. Here there is degenerative change in the joints, narrowing of the disc spaces, and abnormal deposits of bone around the edges of the joints where the pressure has caused calcified tissue to be formed in an attempt at reinforcement. It is often referred to as 'wear and tear' of the joints.

Wear and tear is quite common in the neck joints and the lumbar area of the low back and is sometimes seen in the thoracic spine. It is found in many people from the thirties or forties onwards but in the majority it does not cause any discomfort. Trouble only arises when the muscles and ligaments become stiff or the alignment of the vertebrae is disturbed, bringing increased pressure to one or more of the worn joints.

Spondylitis is a condition in which worn vertebral joints become inflamed. It is more commonly experienced in the neck, causing a good deal of pain, stiffness, and quite often numbness or pins and needles of the fingers and hands owing to pressure on nerve roots in the neck by the bony overgrowths which form around the joint. These symptoms may be aggravated on looking up because the pressure on the facet joints is increased.

Ankylosing spondylitis (Marie-Strumpell disease) is a more advanced form in which the chronically inflamed joints become fused together leading to stiffness and immobility of the spine. The ankylosis usually occurs at the small facet joints which is where most of the degenerative changes are seen.

Rheumatoid arthritis usually affects joints of the extremities such as the shoulders, knees, and fingers, but in severe cases the spinal joints can be involved. Unlike osteoarthritis (OA), which involves only the bone and cartilage, rheumatoid arthritis (RA) affects the surrounding tissues as well. It is a more generalized disease and can attack almost any joint, whereas OA usually develops only in joints which are undergoing repeated friction or injury. Active RA may be detected by blood changes, such as increased sedimentation rate of the red cells.

These conditions can be relieved considerably by improving the circulation to the tissues involved and reducing the body's burden or irritants by reform of your diet. Regularly applied compresses will promote better blood flow; neuromuscular and gentle osteopathic mobilizing loosens joints and relieves pressure; and cleansing diets of fresh raw fruits and vegetables help to reduce tissue acidity which causes inflammation in the joints. You have many ways of overcoming the pain of these conditions without resort to powerful and poisonous drugs.

3. YOUR SELF-HELP PROGRAMME

The practical steps to recovery

Now that you are familiar with your territory of conflict — the muscles, ligaments, bones, and connective tissues of your back — and you understand some of the causes of the discomfort, you can start to devise a programme of relief and rehabilitation. There are many practical procedures by which you can reduce the intensity of your back pain and begin to re-establish normal activity.

What is probably most reassuring is the fact that the greatest contributions to back comfort and recovery come from the measures you can carry out in your own home. You don't need the powerful and expensive new drugs. You don't need costly and complicated equipment. You don't need orthopaedic specialists and neurosurgeons. And, whilst the services of your osteopath or chiropractor may be a valuable part of your recovery programme, the implementation of these self-help measures will certainly make his or her work easier and cut down the number of visits you will need to make.

You probably have, in your home, most of the resources needed for the successful management of your chronic back pain and you will be capable of doing much to alleviate the acute attack. Facilities for rest, gentle exercise, water, warmth, and high quality natural food are the tools you require. They are all available in most homes so you can start to use them straight away.

Help for acute and chronic pain

The main measures in this programme of self-help for back pain apply to both chronic and acute conditions. If you have recurring discomfort and stiffness, with intermittent episodes of pain, you will need to put these steps into practice on a regular basis to bring about gradual improvement in the way you cope.

In acute episodes most of the same measures will be applicable with some modifications. At the end of this book you will find a summary of emergency procedures for acute back pain (see page 178). If you are in discomfort now, turn to this for a digest of the measures which I shall introduce in this chapter and describe more fully in the ones that follow.

Practical measures

The ingredients of your back management programme are a set of practical measures which you can and should undertake even if you only get periodical discomfort. They are:

* rest, relaxation, and sleep
* exercise
* hydrotherapy
* massage
* herbal and homoeopathic medicines
* nutritional considerations
* professional help.

Back pain is a warning sign. It is a warning that all is not well structurally or functionally with the back. If warning signs are ignored further damage is likely to occur sooner or later. You should, therefore, take action on at least some, if not all, of the measures in this list.

Combining forces

There is no single strategy described here which, by itself, will solve your back problem. Even if you seek the professional advice and treatment of an osteopath, chiropractor, physiotherapist, or orthopaedic surgeon, you will still need to use other elements of the programme to get the best results.

You will need rest to relieve pressure on irritated nerves. You will need good nourishment to counteract inflammation and restore connective tissues; you will need hydrotherapy to improve the circulation and enable that nourishment to reach the tissues which need it; and, later, you will need exercise to retrieve muscle strength and re-establish the stability of the spine. The best way of doing all this is to use a combination of treatments.

There are a wide range of options available to you even with these self-help measures and, whilst they may seem tedious and time-consuming, your efforts will be repaid in less pain, improved mobility, and a greater sense of security in the way you approach your daily activities. By treating on several levels you will also increase the chance of success because the integrated approach described here is designed to deal with the different elements of back function.

Some of these self-help measures are a part of wider issues concerned with back disorders. Relaxation techniques, for example, are an invaluable approach to the muscle stiffness which is aggravated by emotional upsets or other stresses. The hydrotherapy application of hot and cold fomentations is probably the safest and most effective form of first aid for back pain, and the role of nutrition, though indirect, has implications not only for the integrity of spinal tissues but for the health of the whole body.

These are all so important that we shall consider them in more detail later but here I will summarize the main measures you can start to put into practice now.

Rest

The first (and often the only) advice which is given to the sufferer of back pain is to lie flat and take pain-killers. The first makes sense and the second may be a necessary evil for a short time, but neither is sensible or scientific in the long run.

It is probably wise to take the weight off over-stressed joints and to rest overworked muscles in the morc acute phases of your back trouble, but this won't achieve much without positive steps to aid recovery. Pain-killers may diminish the intensity of your pain, but they do nothing practical to help healing and they merely poison or damage the system. (Aspirin, for example, often causes bleeding in the stomach and intestines when taken regularly and new evidence suggests that it may be responsible for some haemorrhages in the retina of the eye.) Drugs are a poor option when more effective natural measures can be utilized.

The best position

To relieve back pain the position in which you rest and the quality of the surface on which you lie are, of course, critical. Generally, lying flat will be most comfortable as this relieves the pressure on the joints and discs of the spinal column, but the way in which you lie will be important to the comfort of your back, particularly in the acute stage.

Turn to Chapter 4 for some of the ways in which you can make rest a source of relief for neck and back pain without lying for days on end getting stiffer and stiffer.

Exercise

Many experts believe that the prevalence of back pain is due to insufficient exercise. The fitness and flexibility of muscles and joints depends on regular and reasonably strenuous activity.

You might, therefore, ask 'Can exercise help to cure my back trouble?' The answer is 'No and yes!' Exercise is very definitely out of the question for acute back pain but can be an essential part of the programme to overcome stiffness and regain normal strength in the chronic back disorders. In acute pain of the neck or back there is generally some degree of inflammation, and movement will only exaggerate the probable pressure on nerve roots which may be causing this.

There is another reason why you should not rely on exercise to get you out of trouble, and this applies to chronic back pain as well as to the more acute episodes. Where vertebrae have become locked, the muscles around them go into spasm to prevent movement which might be painful. Usually some of the adjacent vertebrae are also involved, causing an area of limited mobility in the spinal column. Above and below this, the joints may move normally or even excessively to try to make up for the restriction. When you do exercises, the free joints move while the locked ones remain restricted, perhaps becoming even tighter.

Your best guideline on exercise for the back is: if it aggravates the pain don't do it. If, on the other hand, moving about eases the situation, you probably need more regular and systematic exercise to loosen the stiff muscles. A few easy movements on a regular basis will do far more good than an elaborate programme with expensive equipment, but always subject to the caution about restricted vertebrae. Get yourself checked by an osteopath or chiropractor before doing anything too vigorous.

Having ensured that it is appropriate to do them, you may gradually introduce some of the simple exercises given in Chapter 6. Your professional adviser may suggest variations of these which will suit your particular needs.

Hydrotherapy

Most people associate hydrotherapy with exercise in pools but it really means any form of treatment using water. Pool exercises can be extremely valuable but home treatment can bring even greater benefits.

Everyone has hot and cold water in their homes so this means you have one of the most outstanding means of pain relief available, and it isn't just pain relief without healing progress, which is what you get from tablets. Most conventional pain-killers, if they work at all, merely reduce the inflammation or the sensation of pain in the nerves without actually doing anything to change the cause. The home hydrotherapy procedure of hot and cold fomentations achieves results by actually helping the healing process.

The use of hot and cold fomentations is possibly the most effective single self-help measure available to the back pain sufferer. It is also one of the simplest and requires just a little help from one of your family or friends. Sometimes you can even manage to treat yourself.

You will find detailed directions for the use of this minor miracle in Chapter 5. Use them now if you have any aches or pains in the neck or back. You will gain some immediate relief. Other ways in which you can use water to help are also described.

Massage

There can hardly be an aching back that does not appreciate a massage. Only the most sensitive of individuals with acutely inflamed tissues will experience anything but great comfort and a sense of relief from physical contact with warm, pliable hands.

Massage is one of the oldest forms of treatment and sadly it is a greatly neglected one. Massage can be applied at any time to reduce general tensions and relax stiffened muscles but it is a great asset in the management of acute pain. It then needs to be applied with care, especially where tissues are particularly tender, but it can reduce the congestion around restricted joints by promoting the local circulation and drainage. Special areas of congestion or 'trigger points', which may cause a lot of discomfort, can be eased by gentle kneading and stretching.

You will need someone else to do the massage on your own back and detailed instructions for their guidance are given on page 90. To get an idea of how it should feel, though, visit a professionally trained massage therapist. The most effective and well directed massage needs to be done by someone experienced in the art, but most people are capable of learning and applying a few comforting strokes to ease the stiffened muscles of friend or family.

Herbs and homoeopathy

Reliance on conventional drugs such as aspirin and paracetamol tends to make people overlook the safer and surer alternatives available in a wide variety of herbal and homoeopathic preparations. Herbal medicines are prepared from the whole plant, or a part, such as the flower or root, and contain the complex of ingredients found in the natural state. When properly selected they have an excellent safety record

Pain-killers

It is an almost universal habit to reach for the pain-killers when something in the body starts to hurt. People do it virtually without thinking about where or what the pain is, let alone why it is there in the first place.

Pain-killers are no more than their name suggests. They only mask the messages that the body is sending to your brain to say that all is not well. Most act by stopping the nerve impulses for a while. Some suppress inflammation, and yet others may be prescribed as muscle relaxants. At best they may be regarded as a stop-gap measure to confront the ravages of the unbearable acute attack but in any other circumstances they are dangerous on two counts.

By suppressing inflammation, blocking nerve impulses, or reducing muscle tensions without correction of the real causes of the pain, there is a risk of using the back when it is at some mechanical disadvantage and thereby incurring further damage. Inflammation signals spasm of muscles or irritation of nerve roots; muscle spasm is guarding joints which may be painful to move. There is, therefore, a danger that you may do more harm to your back through the false sense of security which pain-killers may induce.

The second danger lies in the nature of the drugs themselves. Many are toxic and harmful if taken in any quantity or over a long period. They merely add to the burden of poisons with which your body has to deal. A person with a weak or stiff back may already be rather unhealthy with a greater than usual level of toxins in the body tissues, without adding further to these problems.

Reserve pain-killers for the last resort. There are many safer ways of treating the back which, although they may not mask the pain as quickly as drugs, actually do something to correct the cause.

and may often prove more beneficial, if a little slower in their actions, than many drugs.

Herbs will help to alter the biochemical imbalances which

cause muscle stiffness and they can promote the functions of liver, kidneys, skin, and bowels — the organs that purify the blood and eliminate waste products which may contribute to rheumatic aches and pains.

Homoeopathic remedies are based on medicinal plants but may also use mineral substances, the difference being that they are prepared as very high dilutions. Sometimes the dilution is so fine that the original substance cannot be detected but it leaves its 'imprint' on the remedy. The higher the dilution, or potency, the more powerful the remedy.

One of the classic homoeopathic remedies is Arnica, which is used for all types of injuries and shocks to the body. It is also very serviceable in aching and stiffness or where a feeling of bruising is a feature of the disorder. Make sure you always have some Arnica tablets handy.

The great thing about the herbal and homoeopathic remedies recommended in this book is that they are all completely free from side-effects. Turn to Chapter 9 for more information on the natural medicines which will help you to ease your aching muscles and joints.

Food and your back

We have established that the way we eat and drink may affect the health of the back: we can either go short of essential nutrients or take in too much clogging and devitalizing food which slowly poisons the tissues. It follows, therefore, that we can use dietary control as a tool in the management of back pain.

Every tissue of our bodies depends on adequate oxygen and good nourishment. Chapter 2 considered the importance of getting a good supply to and from the structures of the spine but this won't help much if the goods delivered are of inferior quality.

A variety of vitamins, minerals, and trace elements are needed by the bones, muscles, and connective tissues to sustain their strength and elasticity. As the years go by and digestive efficiency declines, the levels of major minerals and vitamins may become lower, even if the diet is reasonably good. Other changes in the body, such as alterations of the hormone levels of women at the menopause, can increase the loss of minerals, such as calcium, leading to osteoporosis, a progressive weakening of bone substance, in later years.

One of the basic necessities for the prevention of back pain, and also its treatment, is a good nutritional foundation. A diet of wholesome natural foods provides more of the essential elements to maintain healthy tissues. Refined and synthetic 'junk foods' clog the tissues with impurities and rob the body of vital vitamins and minerals.

Where rheumatic type aches persist, and sometimes during acute attacks in which the connective tissues and muscles are hypersensitive and inflamed, restricting what you eat and drink for a few days may rest the digestion and allow the body to remove impurities and inflammatory waste products. Fasting or cleansing diets are an important way of helping the body through a crisis.

When digestive efficiency has been poor, or where demand for certain vitamins and minerals is greater, it may be necessary to take nutritional supplements for a time to increase the body's reserves. Vitamin C is an important anti-inflammatory agent, for example, and is a vital component of connective tissue. Muscles prone to stiffness and pain may be in need of extra magnesium, while sensitive nerves often benefit by supplements of potassium compounds and vitamin B.

In Chapter 8 we shall consider the ways in which you can use the latest knowledge of nutritional science to help you to deal with your back pain more effectively.

Professional help

Although this book is mainly intended to tell you how you can treat your own back problems, it does not rule out the need for professional opinions and treatment. Indeed, it should be positively encouraged in anything but the mildest aches — and then only if they clear up after a few days of the self-help measures described here.

It is important to find out exactly what is causing your back pain in order to be able to treat it in the most effective manner. Vertebral displacements, disturbances of muscle balance, and inadequacies of the nourishment and energy of muscles and connective tissue may all need the various skills of practitioners to help restore better balance in back function. Practitioners with the appropriate expertise are able to correct the problems, such as locking of the joints, which will not respond to rest, compresses, and other self-help measures. You will still need to do your homework. It complements the professional attention you may receive, and by working at it you will make the task of the practitioner that much more speedy and effective.

Various professional options available to you are described in Chapter 13. In general, the first opinion of any back or neck trouble should be sought from an osteopath or chiropractor who will decide whether referral to other specialists is necessary.

An integrated approach

There is no single answer to back and neck pain. So many factors may be involved, a number of which are interdependent, so you cannot rely on just one form of help. That is why people are often disappointed when they have tried one type of treatment without much success. Important supportive factors may have been neglected which help to make a treatment more effective.

Osteopathic correction of vertebral misalignments, for example, cannot have lasting results if the muscles and ligaments are not properly balanced. Surgical fusion of badly damaged joints will not bring back the strength and tone of the back muscles without a well-designed programme of exercises and good nutrition. Bed rest will not bring much relief without the powerful circulation-promoting benefits of hot and cold fomentations.

Your best prospects for healthy back maintenance lie in the integrated approach described here. Now you are familiar with the main options available to you we shall look at some of the more valuable self-help measures in more detail.

4. REST AND RELAXATION

Reducing the burden of back pain

The pendulum of opinion as to whether it is better to move or rest the wayward back has swung to and fro for many years and shows no sign of coming to a halt at either end of its curve. There are those who believe the only way to overcome back pain is to stretch and loosen and strengthen it by vigorous exercise, and those who advocate inactivity and rest for long periods. People have been driven through a form of purgatory in the cause of the former and encased in plaster for weeks by exponents of the latter.

As it happens there is some value in the less extreme applications of both schools of thought, but it depends very much on the nature and intensity of the back pain. The chronically stiff, intermittently aching back needs regular movement to maintain mobility but, where there is acute pain and inflammation with irritation of nerve roots, rest is essential.

Movement, though, must be done with the necessary cautions, to avoid aggravating areas of wear or injury, and rest, likewise, must be used in ways which will help the healing process and not merely let your muscles and joints stagnate and seize up.

When rest is a must

These are the situations in which rest is essential:

* any pain of sudden onset
* acute pain located in one area
* pain which radiates down an arm or leg
* pain which is aggravated by movement.

Obviously there are borderline situations. Sometimes there may be stiffness which can be eased by movement initially, but after a time pain arises from irritation of the nerves near misaligned joints. Since most pains are caused by pressure on nerves or movement of irritated or bruised tissues, immobilization is necessary but it is also important to rest in a position which will minimize any compression of the offending joints. This nearly always means lying flat as only then is the effect of gravity on disc spaces and facet joints removed.

When you lie flat the fibrous tissue of the intervertebral discs can begin to absorb fluid and the synovial membranes

Fig 9 Your resting surface should give firm support

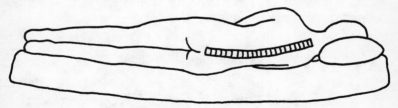

WRONG – uneven support causes stress on the spine

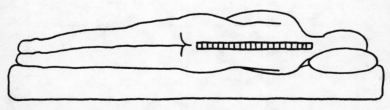

RIGHT – firm support keeps spine straight but yields to the prominent shoulders and hips

of the facet joints, free of the friction of the movement, can receive more blood and regain some of their nourishment.

The position in which you need to lie may vary according to the area and the type of pain and it is also necessary to have the right surface on which to rest.

The right surface for rest

The surface on which you lie needs to be firm but comfortable. There should not be any excessive sagging or sinking of the mattress which could cause stress or uneven pressures at certain points in the spine. It needs to be soft enough to allow the prominent parts of your body, such as buttocks or hips, to sink in a little whilst keeping the spinal column in its natural relaxed position. (See Fig 9.)

The ideal is to have a fairly firm mattress on a fixed base. If your bed has a sprung base it may be better to place the mattress on the floor but a board placed on the divan under the mattress may also provide the necessary stability.

The best position

The part of the back which is affected by pain may dictate the requirements for rest and certainly the position you should adopt for maximum comfort.

Fig 10 Support the knees and hips when lying flat

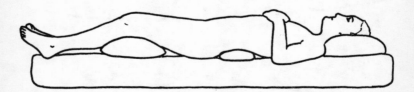

Low back pain

For most types of pain you will find that lying on the back is the best position. It may help to place a pillow or bolster under your knees. This reduces any exaggeration of the backward curve and relieves pressure on the facet joints of the lower lumbar vertebrae and where the sciatic nerve roots pass out. It reduces the pain which is concentrated across the centre of the lower back.

You may also experiment with a thin pillow, or rolled up hand-towel, beneath the small of the back. This can be helpful in pain which is more diffuse in the area of the lower back or is associated with narrowing of the disc spaces. You will need to work out the best position. For example, if your pain is fairly low on the lumbo-sacral junction just above the buttocks, you should place the wedge right beneath the base of the spine just at the top of the buttocks; but if you have more discomfort towards the waist it may help to lift slightly below the lower ribs. With the support in position try to relax and release the pain.

Pain in the legs

Pain or numbness which affects one leg generally suggests pressure on the roots of the nerves leaving the spinal cord on the same side. They are squeezed by the congested tissues caused by contracted muscles and narrowing of the aperture between the vertebrae where the nerve passes from the spinal cord. In these cases the side lying position may afford more relief. By lying on the side to which pain radiates you stretch the spine, and pressure on the nerve roots may be relieved.

Neck and upper back

The pains of the neck and upper back are not so much the result of compression but may, nevertheless, be relieved by rest. The weight borne by the vertebrae in the neck is much less and they are proportionately smaller, but they do have a wider range of movement which causes its own problems.

Wear and tear or displacement of vertebrae in the neck can create pressure in the nerves issuing from that level and the surrounding tissues may soon become inflamed. Then even quite small movements are painful and rest is essential.

Pain between the shoulders

Pain in the thoracic area of the spine, usually between the shoulder blades, can be the consequence of either arthritis or vertebral restriction and muscle spasm. If there is vertebral restriction the bones are commonly bent back on each other with contraction of the muscles on either side of the spine so a position of rest which tends to reverse that restriction may help.

Lie flat on the back but place a small wedge pillow under the lumbar vertebrae and another in the nape of the neck. This allows the area between the shoulders to sag a little and stretches the tight muscles.

If resting makes it worse

There are some cases of acute low back pain for whom lying aggravates the pain. This is very much a matter of the pressure by inflamed tissues on specific nerve roots being increased in a particular position. Perhaps the angle of the facet joints when you lie on your back is aggravating this situation. It may help to experiment with pillows as described above to find a position which relieves the pressure.

Some of the pain following rest is due to a build-up of congestion which disperses once the blood moves a little more freely with activity.

Collars

Some people are prescribed a collar, a firm piece of padded polystyrene or plastic, which minimizes the movement of the head and neck. This can be quite a useful expedient for a short time in cases of acute neck pain but does nothing to help recovery. If you use a collar be certain to take other treatments, such as hydrotherapy or osteopathy, to correct the disorder.

Pillows

When lying in bed a stiff or painful neck will appreciate a minimal amount of well-placed support. Throw out your bolster or second pillow (unless you need to use it under your knees) and ensure that the remaining pillow is not too thick, for you need to lie as flat as possible. A soft down or feather pillow which can be shaped to the nape of your neck will be best. If you lie on your back, shape the pillow to support the head reasonably in line with your body. If you are a side-lier bunch it up to fill the space between head and shoulders. Either way the spine should remain reasonably straight.

Specially shaped neck pillows are worthy of trial. More information on these is given in Chapter 12.

Relaxation and sleep

Having found a comfortable position in which to rest the next thing is to relax and let go of your pain. A lot of the tension associated with back pain is due to guarding — holding your muscles tense to prevent a movement which may give you a sharp twinge. The trouble is, the more you tighten the stiffer you become and the more likely you are to have pain. It is difficult to avoid tensing when you are standing and moving about but learning to let go when you rest can be an essential prerequisite to sound sleep.

Turn to page 139 for more details of relaxation routines you can use both to release the physical spasms which are locking your back and to reduce the tension and anxieties which may have contributed more than you realize to the discomfort you feel. Once you can reduce tension and pain, sleep will probably follow without difficulty.

Sleep is vital to healing and regeneration. During sleep the stress hormones, which are normally plentiful in the body during waking hours, give way to the powerful growth hormone which helps to counteract inflammation and replaces damaged tissues.

If you have difficulty sleeping, a simple hydrotherapy procedure is to bathe the lower legs and feet in cold water for 2–3 minutes before retiring. Use the bathroom spray attachment or sponge the legs with cold water then dab them dry before getting into bed.

5. THE WATER WONDER-CURE

Hydrotherapy in the home

It is the most widely available substance on earth. It is essential to life. It is possibly the single most effective tool for the relief of pain and yet it is probably the most neglected. It is water.

Water is abundantly accessible in most modern homes and that means the homes of people in whom backache is most prevalent. Back pain is a product of a modern life style. Although we know that primitive people had arthritic degeneration — quite noticeable degenerative changes are to be seen in some skeletons from the Iron Age and earlier — we can assume that they were not without the odd ache or pain. But it is the 'civilized' comforts of cars, soft couches, and convenience foods that are conducive to back problems.

Inadequate physical activity, coupled with poor quality nourishment, creates or encourages a premature deterioration in the strength and tone of the spinal structures. Water provides one way to restore vitality and speed up the dispersal of inflammatory waste products from the tissues. Everyone who has used its simple application by hot and cold fomentations will have no hesitation in regarding water as the real wonder-cure.

The working liquid

Water has a number of properties which make it not only essential to life but outstanding as a healing agent.

As a liquid it is capable of carrying a number of vital vitamins and minerals and medicinal herbs, which it can dissolve. Vitamins B and C and minerals such as calcium, magnesium, manganese, and zinc are transported to the muscles and connective tissues by the blood in a water-soluble form. Waste products from these same tissues are carried away in solution to be eliminated by kidneys, lungs, bowels, and skin. Water can also change its form: it can become solid by freezing, and vaporize when heated. Both these properties may be used therapeutically but it is in its liquid form that it is of greatest value to the back pain sufferer. In this form it can take up heat or cold and transmit it to and from the body surface.

The skin

The medium through which your body responds to hydrotherapy applications is the skin. It is one of your most active and important organs.

The skin protects your body from the external environment but is also designed to help you to interact with it. The pores, through which you sweat, and a rich supply of blood vessels enable you to regulate your body temperature when that around you is changing. Perspiration is also an important method of elimination of impurities — the 'silt' that may build up in rheumatism and muscular stiffness.

You can also make use of the skin's property of absorption. It can actively take up minerals and medicinal compounds dissolved in water with which it is in contact or from ointments and creams. The fame of many spas is based on the fact that people derive benefit from the ionized minerals present in the local water in which they bathe.

The main way in which the skin is involved in your back treatment is by its response to contrasts of temperature.

How hot and cold fomentations help

The benefits of hot and cold fomentations applied with towels or similar materials are both mechanical and physiological. The hot application dilates the blood vessels and draws heat to the skin surface, encouraging relaxation. It is, therefore, comforting for muscle stiffness but may aggravate congestion and inflamed tissues if used without the cold compress.

The contrast of the cold application induces a contraction of the capillaries and small vessels on the surface so blood is shunted away from the congested and inflamed tissues. The shunted blood carries away waste products of inflammation but then — and this is the important part — this action is followed by the body's reaction which is to send in fresh oxygenated blood to bathe these tissues. Better circulation is established by repeating the process so it is important always to finish with cold, particularly in any areas where there may be inflammation, such as around irritated nerve roots.

Apart from increasing the blood supply to painful tissues, the promotion of circulation enables the skin to work more efficiently as an organ of elimination.

No substitutes

There are several other ways of applying contrasting temperatures to painful areas but there are no substitutes in terms of effectiveness for the towels.

Standing under the shower and using alternating hot and cold jets may help but is not so effective. Likewise, hot water bottles, bags of frozen peas, or the special plastic packs which can be heated up in the oven or cooled in the fridge, are all of limited value; to ease stiffness, in the case of the heat, or reduce inflammation, in the case of the cold applications. None of these work in quite the same way as the fomentations.

The immediate contact of the moist heat or cold with the skin promotes a better response. Also the surface vessels can react to the cold compresses. Ice bags or frozen peas merely prolong the chilling effect and prevent the vitally important reaction of the skin as fresh blood flows back.

How to apply hot and cold fomentations

All you need are two small towels and access to hot and cold water. The towels need only be large enough, when folded two or three times, to cover the painful area. If this is the low back the folded towel will need to cover about 8in. x 10in. (20cm x 25cm). Most areas higher up the back will need less. Fomentations can, of course, be applied to the full length of the spine with a larger towel.

If a member of your family or a friend can apply the fomentations for you, lie face downwards on the bed with your abdomen over a pillow. This will stretch the muscles of the lower back slightly and decrease the pressure on the facet joints and the back of the intervertebral disc which is usually under the greatest pressure. If the pain is in the neck or shoulders you can be treated sitting up. You may also be able to apply the fomentations to your lower back yourself whilst sitting on a stool by the wash-basin. The only part you will be unable to reach yourself is the upper back between the shoulders.

Soak the first towel in hot water, then wring it out well. Tap water should be hot enough. The towel may be folded and rolled up while it is being squeezed out. This prevents scalding the operator's hands. The towel is then unrolled so that the inner, hotter surface can be placed on the affected area of the back. Use two or three layers' thickness of the towel. This should be left in place for about three minutes.

Meanwhile the second towel is prepared in a similar way using cold water, again from the tap. As soon as the hot fomentation is removed the cold one is put in its place for a duration of one minute.

Then repeat the sequence — *three minutes hot, one minute cold, three minutes hot, one minute cold* — for about twenty minutes, or even longer if there is acute back pain.

When to use hot and cold fomentations

Hot and cold fomentations may be applied any time you feel stiffness or pain in your back. They are particularly effective for relief of acute pain and should then be applied several times a day for twenty to thirty minutes at a time. Fomentations play an invaluable role in the management of severe pain. Used in conjunction with bed rest, regular fomentations can speed the process of recovery.

For chronic backache regular applications of hot and cold towels is also of great benefit. A session last thing at night can help you to get up in the morning with a little less stiffness. If you are having regular osteopathy, chiropractic, or acupuncture treatment hot and cold fomentations will increase the benefit you derive from it.

Hot baths

Hot baths are a source of comfort for many sufferers from chronic back pain. They reduce the stiffness of the muscles and joints by increasing the flow of blood through the affected areas.

Epsom salts baths

The addition of a double handful of commercial Epsom salts (magnesium sulphate) to the water helps to increase the action. Soaking in the hot Epsom salts bath opens the pores and induces perspiration which carries out impurities. According to Chinese medicine, sweating enables the body to expel the cold or damp factors which may have penetrated the muscles after physical work in the wind or wet weather.

You may soak in a hot Epsom salts bath for up to twenty minutes. If you perspire freely it would be wise to place a cold compress on your forehead to prevent lightheadedness. Before you get out of the bath, which you must do slowly, rinse or sponge down with cool or tepid water to close the pores and balance the circulation. You may not be able to wash with soap in an Epsom salts bath as it hardens the water. Some proprietary bath salts are basically magnesium sulphate with softeners.

Herbal baths

As the skin is an active absorbant of medicinal substances in solution, herbal baths are a beneficial and pleasant way of treating back pain and rheumatism.

Medicinal herbs can be added to bath water either as ready prepared decoctions and infusions, or by placing the dried or crushed herbs in the bath directly. If the latter method is used the herbs may be placed in a muslin or cheesecloth bag which should be hung from the tap to allow the hot water to rinse through as you run the bath. Wring out the bag to extract the juices and then place it in the bath water to steep. Liquid extracts of herbs or powdered dry herbs may also be added to the water for a hot bath.

Herbal baths may be used for their stimulant properties to promote circulation and elimination, using plants such as basil, bay, lavender, pine, or rosemary, or to relax muscles and nerves, using catnip, chamomile, or lime flowers (see page 128) for more detail on medicinal herbs for the back). Sebastian Kneipp, the nineteenth century Bavarian priest, is regarded as the father of hydrotherapy and in his famous book *My Water Cure* (Society of Metaphysicians, 1986) he suggests the use of oat-straw infusion in the bath for treatment of rheumatism. Oatmeal can be mixed with other herbal ingredients.

Another classic for medicinal baths is bran. Bran baths may also be used for their cleansing and relaxing properties. Add a heaped double handful of oat- or wheat-bran to the bath water and stir it in.

Essential oils of medicinal herbs may be added to the bath water. Only a few drops of these oils need to be added as they are quite powerful (see Aromatherapy, Chapter 9).

Soak in therapeutic baths for twenty to thirty minutes. If you perspire, a cold compress should be applied to the forehead to prevent lightheadedness on rising from the bath.

Sitz-baths

The sitz-bath is a contrasting hip bath which is tonic to the abdominal, pelvic, and low back areas. Sitz-baths originated in the German spas where hydrotherapy is widely used. Proper sitz-baths require specially designed hip baths but you can improvise with a large bowl or baby bath in your main bath tub. Place tolerably hot water in the bowl and cold water in the bath. The bowl of hot water can be placed in the bath.

Sit in the hot water with your feet in the cold water for three minutes. Then change round to sit in the cold water with your feet in the bowl of hot water for one minute. (A better way, of course, is to have two large bowls and sit in them alternately). Repeat the procedure three times, massaging the hips and lower abdomen while you are bathing.

The contrast bathing benefits the low back area and the improvement of abdominal circulation encourages proper bowel and kidney function, aiding detoxification.

6. EXERCISE

To move or not to move

There is *exercise* and there are *exercises* and both are essential in coping with chronic back pain.

Exercise means activity, sports and pastimes which entail a variety of movements — the most pleasant and, generally, most suitable way of keeping your joints supple, provided common sense precautions are applied in the way you do them.

Exercises are the specific movements you perform to loosen stiff joints or strengthen weak muscles. They require determination, dedication, and discipline because, if they are to achieve results, they must be performed regularly and accurately.

There are also exercise systems such as yoga, T'ai chi, and Qi gong which maintain harmony of body energy and postural flexibility in the spine.

Exercise is, therefore, a big subject and in this chapter I shall review the most useful approaches for the person with chronic back pain and give guidelines on sporting activities and pastimes.

Strengthening or stretching

There are two main schools of thought regarding the objectives of exercise for the back. There are those who champion a rigorous routine designed to strengthen the muscles of the spine and other postural muscles, such as those of the thighs, while others advocate an approach which will stretch the muscles and loosen the joints.

The 'strengtheners' argue, quite logically, that the muscles and joints must be trained to cope with the everyday demands of work and play. In most cases back trouble arises from the lack of tone in the tissues and poor circulation and nourishment that is the consequence of the relative inactivity of modern life.

With this principle in mind, Dr Tom Mayer, a former orthopaedic surgeon, established the Productive Rehabilitation Institute of Dallas for Ergonomics (PRIDE) in Texas. This provides an intensive twelve-week programme of exercise, counselling, and occupational therapy, performing the kinds of tasks the subject would do at work. An elaborate piece of exercise equipment, called the 'Iron Maiden', which measures the strength and endurance of the back and abdominal muscles, is a major feature of this programme. This is linked to a computer which assesses and monitors the progress of the patients. According to one report, 87 per cent of patients who complete the PRIDE programme returned to work and were still working two years later. According to the *Observer Magazine* (3 July 1988) which described the PRIDE experiment, specialists hope to establish similar programmes in the United Kingdom.

Such a vigorous system requires tremendous commitment, motivation, and self-discipline. Having established more stability in the spine it is necessary to keep up a regular programme of exercise to prevent further long-term decline but this is a rule for anyone with chronic back pain — careful maintenance and sensible use will always be necessary to keep out of trouble.

A significant number of back pains, however, are the consequence of excessive muscular stiffness and restricted motion in spinal joints. They will respond better to carefully selected movements and stretching procedures, but even these may not be of great value if the specific area of disturbance has not been professionally treated. Launching into a vigorous exercise programme without correction of the areas of fixation in the spine will only compound the problem. Remember that when these trouble spots are neglected, exercise merely loosens the free joints on either side while the tight spot gets tighter. Strengthening exercises merely bind them even more.

The success of any exercise depends on selecting the right system for your type of problem. The tough training programme of the Texas team can only be judged by the kind of people who take it in the first place. Physically active, highly motivated people are more likely to complete such an arduous programme (which will also bias the results). But back pain afflicts people of all shapes and sizes, of varying strengths and weaknesses, and of diverse determination and will-power.

Adjusting the guy ropes

When a group of vertebrae become restricted in their range of motion it is usually in a position of forwards, backwards, or side-bending, and rotation, depending on which level of the spinal column is affected. There may, for example, be a flattening of the normal backward curve of the lumbar spine and often with this goes a loss of the forward curve in the thoracic region. In other words the lumbar vertebrae are bent forwards, compressing the discs, and the thoracic vertebrae are bent backwards, increasing pressure on the facet joints. When this happens there is a contraction of the muscles on the side to which the bones have bent and a stretching of those on the outer side of the curve. To use the guy rope analogy, one side is too tight and the other is too slack.

The balance of the low back and pelvis will also depend on the elasticity of the long thigh muscles. The front muscles of the thigh, the quadriceps, pull the pelvis forwards which increases the angle of the lumbo-sacral joint; in other words, it tilts the sacrum back. Weakness of the front muscles of the abdominal wall also increases this tendency. The sagging 'beer gut' is often accompanied by an exaggerated lumbar curve. Contraction of the hamstring muscles, at the back of the thighs, tends to tuck the bottom in and flatten the lumbar spine. (See Fig 11.)

Most muscles can be seen in outline or felt beneath the skin but there is one that often goes unnoticed and is usually neglected because it lies at the back of the abdominal cavity in front of the spinal column, called *iliopsoas*. There is one on each side, and they can only be felt through the abdominal wall of slimmer subjects, but it is a very important postural muscle. Iliopsoas commonly becomes contracted, pulling the lower back into the forward bending position.

To achieve a more comfortable balance in the spine these muscles may need strengthening or stretching. A muscle which needs to contract and shorten is called an *agonist*, while those which oppose it are the *antagonists*.

Fig 11 Postural muscles

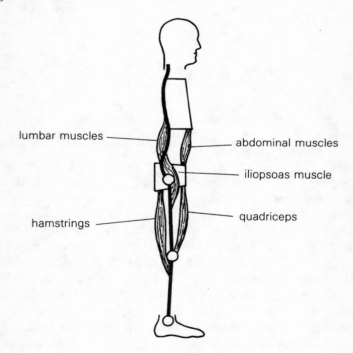

lumbar muscles

abdominal muscles

iliopsoas muscle

hamstrings

quadriceps

Which type of exercise?

When it comes to choosing exercises for rehabilitation of the back it pays to keep them simple. You don't want a complicated or time-consuming chore on which you may soon give up because of boredom. A few very simple movements

Stretch the strong to strengthen the weak

It was long believed that to strengthen the back the weakened agonist muscles should be exercised, but experts now believe that strengthening, while of the utmost importance, is best achieved not by working the weak muscles but by stretching the strong ones which antagonize them — in other words, making use of the guy rope principle. This allows the agonist muscle to take up its slack and become shorter. We stretch the strong to strengthen the weak.

You can use this principle in your exercise programme. The new muscle energy techniques practised by many osteopaths and chiropractors use a stretch and hold method which allows the nerve impulses to the muscle fibres to change. These may be incorporated into some sensible exercises while others may require gentle movement to loosen joints or stretch ligaments.

which help to loosen the joints and stretch the muscles which most need it are more likely to become a regular part of your day's routine.

Avoid exercises which involve swings, bounces, and jerks — the sort in which you twist the trunk round to the limit of its movement and then swing back to the other side as far as you can go. As you reach the end of the range of movement the joints are forced into a position of locking and the force of the swing stretches ligaments beyond their normal limits. Instead of making the back more flexible there will be an unnecessary torsional stress on particular areas which could create problems later. Keep exercises smooth and gentle.

Restoring the balance

The selection of exercises described here are chosen to work on the major postural muscles and will help to restore the balance of your spinal joints.

Don't attempt to do everything: select the two or three most likely to balance your particular trouble spot. If it is the upper back and shoulders, the *head roll* and *shoulder shrug* will be sufficient; for the low back area with exaggerated curve you may need only the *lumbar stretch* and the *abdominal exercise*; for the flattened lumbar curve in which the lower back sags backwards when seated, the *psoas stretch* will be needed.

If performed correctly these exercises are gentle and harmless, but bear in mind that individual requirements for particular parts of the back may vary so if in doubt about the suitability of any routine do seek professional advice. There are, in any case, certain precautions which must be observed.

Precautions for exercise

* Do not attempt to exercise when you have acute pain of the neck or back.
* Do not exercise if you have sharp pain or numbness in the extremities.
* Do not perform any exercise which increases the pain.
* Do not perform any exercises which involve swings or jerks (none of those in this book do).

When and where to perform your exercises

The ideal place to do your exercises is on a soft mat on the floor. An exercise mat or a folded rug will do. You will need a firm base but not so hard that you bruise your bones in the process!

The best time is first thing in the morning as your joints and muscles will appreciate the loosening effect, although you may find that some movements are easier to perform later in the day. Some of the neck and shoulder exercises can be repeated at any time of the day, for example at the office.

Wear pyjamas or loose clothing, such as shorts or a track suit.

Exercises for the neck and back

All exercises should be done slowly and smoothly without any vigorous swinging and jerking to the limit of your range of movement. Observe the precautions when performing your exercise but don't be afraid of some creaking and crunching from thickened muscle fibres and stiff joints. These noises are harmless and invariably occur after a period of inactivity.

Fig 12 Head rolling

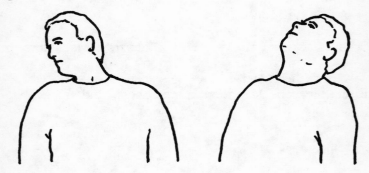

Neck and shoulders

Head rolling
Stand or sit upright, arms at the side, shoulders relaxed. Allow the head to bend to one side then let it roll slowly backwards in a wide arc towards the other shoulder. Then let it roll forwards and round to the side you started with. Turn your face towards the side to which the head is rolling. Rather than pulling the head round let it fall by releasing the neck muscles on the side opposite to which it is rolling. (See Fig 12.)

As you rotate backwards breathe in slowly, and as you roll forwards breathe out. Repeat this rotation six times then change to circle in the opposite direction. This exercise may be performed two or three times a day as you go about your duties at home or in the office.

Effect: all-round release of neck muscles and joints.

Side turning
Stand or sit upright with arms and shoulders relaxed. Turn the head slowly to look over your right shoulder and then return to face forwards and continue the move to look over your left shoulder.

Repeat six times, breathing in as you turn the head and out as it moves to the front. Perform this movement two or three times a day.

Effect: stretches neck and upper back muscles.

Shoulder shrugging

Standing comfortably with feet apart, arms relaxed at your sides. Move the shoulders backwards in a slow rolling shrug. The tips of the shoulders should each describe as wide a circle as possible. (See Fig 13.)

Do six backward circles then six forwards. Make sure the arms stay loose by the sides and don't let them get actively involved in the exercise.

Effect: loosens shoulder, upper chest, and upper back muscles.

Fig 13 Shoulder shrugging

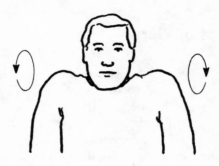

Upper and middle back

Thoracic stretch

Sit on a chair or stool with the feet squarely placed. Place your hands as far as possible around the opposite shoulder so that you are hugging yourself. Drop your head forwards.

Bend forwards towards your knees as far as possible. Allow gravity to take you so that you have a sense of hanging in that position. Try not to bend the lower back. You should feel a stretch or pull on the muscles on either side of the thoracic spine. Now breathe in and straighten just a little way, then hold your breath whilst maintaining the position for seven to

Fig 14 Thoracic stretch

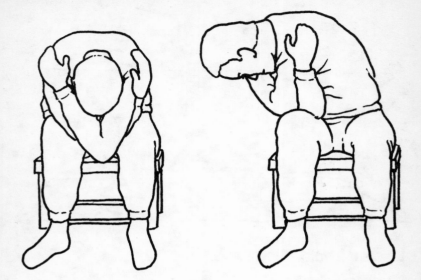

ten seconds. As you breathe out again drop forwards to a full stretch. Repeat this three times. (See Fig 14.)

Now repeat the exercise with a turn to the right side as you bend forwards; straighten and turn to the left. This is a continuous movement repeated six times without holding one position.

Effect: stretches muscles of upper back between the shoulder blades.

Thoracic extension

Lie face downwards on the floor or exercise mat with your face to one side. Place your hands palms downwards beside your head with your elbows tucked in at your side.

Push down slightly on your hands and forearms as you raise the head and upper body backwards. Keep your hips in contact with the floor but stretch back as far as you can breathing in as you do so. Lower again, breathing out, and rest your face on the other side. Repeat six times. (Fig 15.)

Effect: stretches the ligaments at the front of the spinal column and opens up the excessive forward bend of the thoracic vertebrae.

Fig 15 Thoracic extension

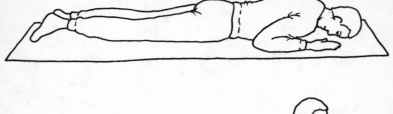

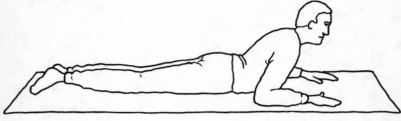

Lower back

Lumbar stretch

Lie on your back on a firm but comfortable surface. A folded blanket or exercise mat would be suitable.

Draw up both knees towards your chest and clasp your hands around them with fingers interlaced or gripping. Pull your knees towards your chest to stretch the lower back. Hold for seven to ten seconds and then relax and repeat three times. (See Fig 16.)

Relax for a moment and then repeat this position but now, with the tops of the knees, describe as wide a circle as you can without rolling over. Repeat six times clockwise and six times anticlockwise.

Fig 16 Lumbar stretch

Effect: as you pull the knees in an arc towards the chest, the muscles and ligaments of the lumbo-sacral area are stretched and the joints are loosened.

Lumbar roll

Lie on your back on a firm but comfortable surface. Draw your feet up to rest flat on the floor close to your buttocks with knees bent. Keep the knees together and allow them to fall to the right and then over to the left. As you do this movement try to keep the feet and the shoulders in contact with the floor. Repeat three times in each direction. (See Fig 17.)

Effect: stretches the muscles and loosens the joints of the lumbar and lower thoracic spine.

Fig 17 Lumbar roll

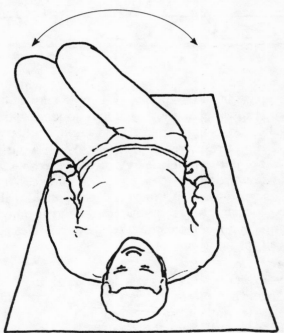

Abdominal tone

Lie flat on your back on an exercise mat. Bend your knees with the feet flat on the floor close to your buttocks. Clasp your hands behind your neck. As you curl the head forwards onto the chest, continue the movement until your back is partially off the floor whilst pushing down with the feet and pressing back towards the buttocks with the heels. This last manoeuvre prevents contraction of the iliopsoas muscle so that the exercise can concentrate on the rectus abdominis muscles at the front of the abdominal wall. Lower to the floor and repeat six times. (See Fig 18.)

Fig 18 Abdominal tone

Sacral rock

(This exercise is suitable only for people with quite flexible knees and hips.) Squat down on your haunches with your feet 9–12 inches (25–30 cm) apart flat on the floor. Let your arms stretch out and rest over your knees to help your balance.

Now rock gently from one foot to the other, allowing your pelvis to sway from side to side. You should keep the feet flat on the floor. Repeat ten times in each direction. (Fig 19.)

Effect: loosens the sacro-iliac joints and ligaments at the base of the spine and stretches the soleus muscles at the base of the calf in the lower leg.

Lumbar tone

Lie on your front, head to one side, arms at the side with the palms downwards. Raise the left leg backwards off the floor keeping it straight. Lift to about twenty degrees, then lower it. Now raise and lower the right leg in a similar fashion. Repeat six times, alternating legs. (See Fig 20.)

Effect: strengthens the lumbar muscles to overcome excessive forward bending of the low back area.

Psoas stretch (warrior position)

Stand with feet about 9–12 inches (25–30cm) apart with the

Fig 19 Sacral rock

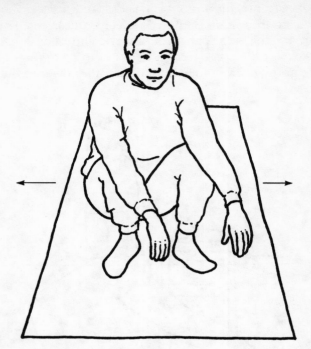

Fig 20 Lumbar tone

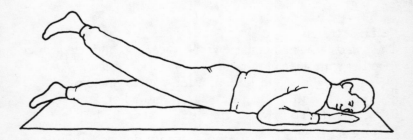

back of a chair at your left side for support if necessary. Put the left hand on the back of the chair, and reach forward as far as possible with the right foot, stretching the left leg behind you. Keep the feet pointing forwards. Drop into the fencing lunge position with the right knee bent. Return to resting position. (See Fig 21.)

Now turn the other way and grip the chair with the right hand. Reach forward with the left foot and stretch the right thigh backwards. Repeat the complete process five times.

Effect: stretches the psoas muscle at the front of the lumbar spine.

Fig 21 Psoas stretch

Soleus stretch

The *soleus* is a small muscle at the lower end of the leg which, together with the calf muscles (the gastrocnemiae), is inclined to become shortened and prevent you from being able to squat down with the feet flat. This contraction is most likely to occur in people who habitually wear high heels. The following exercise may help to stretch these muscles.

Stand facing a wall about 3–4ft (90–120cm) away. Rest your hands against the wall and then stretch forward with your left leg, keeping the right leg straight with the toes pointing forwards. Keep the back straight and reach forward until you feel the stretch at the back of the lower right leg. Hold this position for five to seven seconds. Step back and repeat the exercise leading with the right leg. Repeat six times. (Fig 22.)

Fig 22 Soleus stretch

Thigh stretchers

Rectus femoris is the large muscle at the front of the thigh which maintains postural balance. The following exercise will help to stretch this if it is shortened.

   Stand beside a chair and hold onto this with your left hand. Raise your right leg, bend it as far as you can and grip the ankle with your right hand. Pull the right heel back towards your buttock keeping the thigh in a straight line with the body. Breathe in as you do so and hold the breath while you try to retain this position against the resistance of the leg for five to ten seconds. Breathe out and pull your heel further towards the buttock to stretch the muscle before relaxing. Repeat with the left leg. Perform this exercise three times on each side. (Fig 23.)

Fig 23 Rectus stretch

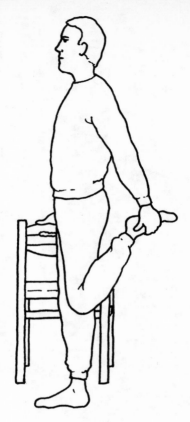

The *hamstrings* are the group of muscles at the back of the thigh. To stretch these the following simple exercise can be performed.

Place your left heel on a lowish stool and, with this leg straight, slowly bend the right knee to stretch the hamstrings. Hold for five seconds then release. Repeat with the right leg raised while bending the left leg. Keep your back straight while you perform this exercise. You may need to hold onto a chair for support while you are doing it. (Fig 24.)

Tensor fascia latae is a small muscle at the side of the hip which extends to the knee as a band of fibrous tissue. It often becomes tight, giving pain in the hip and thigh. The following exercise helps to stretch it and balance the pelvis.

Fig 24 Hamstring stretch

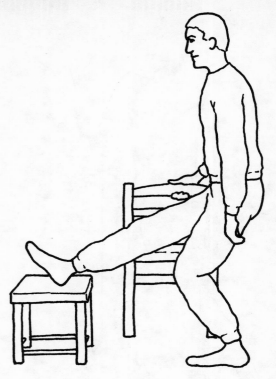

Stand sideways on to a wall with the left arm outstretched, hand resting on the wall. Cross your right leg in front of the left. Keeping your left leg straight, bend the right knee towards the wall until your left forearm is resting against the wall. Repeat three times then do the same on the other side. (Fig 25.)

Exercise for pleasure

The bend and curl type of exercises are designed for specific areas of the spine. They could be described as necessity exercises. General exercise is what you do primarily for pleasure and the feeling of well-being it induces — active pastimes, sports, and games. It also plays a valuable role in health maintenance generally but is of particular benefit to the back.

Fig 25 Tensor fascia stretch

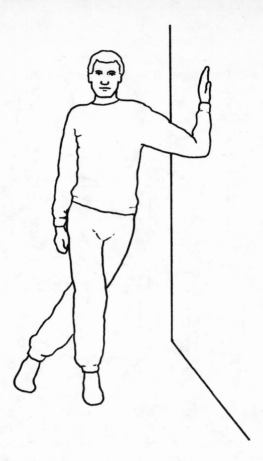

The first essential of general exercise is that you should enjoy doing it. It is no good going for a three mile jog every morning if you regard it as a chore; you may be better off weeding
the garden or walking the dog. Far better to do something you
can look forward to.

Most activities are beneficial but there are drawbacks to
some. Badminton, tennis, squash, or golf are all of value
although very one-sided. Swimming and walking are two of
the finest exercises. They are bilateral and, if performed
regularly and rhythmically, help to maintain the flexibility of
the spine and its muscles.

Remember that these are ways of keeping well not just for your back but on every level, but if you have an old injury, such as a prolapsed disc with degenerative changes, you must respect your limitations. Choose activities which don't impose excessive compressive forces on vulnerable joints.

As with most exercise it is far better to do a moderate amount — say twenty minutes daily — than longer, less frequent bouts.

Walking

Brisk walking is one of the finest ways of keeping fit. If you are able to stride out with a good rhythm the back muscles contract and relax as the weight shifts from one leg to another. The gentle undulations of the spinal column squeeze the discs and encourage the interchange of fluids which are so important for their nourishment.

Good foot care and suitable footwear are essential for walking. Corns, callouses, or pinching shoes will cause limps which destabilize the spine and lead to stress and strain.

Running and jogging

Whilst running and jogging are good for heart and lungs they are not so good for backs. The impact of running on hard surfaces, such as pavements and roads, sends shock waves through the legs to the spine which repeatedly jars joints that are worn and increases the compression of the intervertebral discs, especially when they have degenerated.

If you enjoy jogging, try to do it on grass and wear good quality, well-cushioned shoes which can absorb some of the impact. Barefoot running in sand is also effective without being too traumatic to the spine. You can jog on the spot with a rebound exerciser, a mini-trampoline, which avoids the jarring you would get from hard surfaces.

Cycling

No impact on the spinal joints occurs with cycling but it is rather an unnatural position to hold for too long if you use drop handlebars. The prolonged forward bending of the thoracic and lumbar spine compresses the discs, while the backward inclination of the neck imposes pressure on the facet joints of the cervical vertebrae. This is not so good with low back problems or arthritic wear in the neck. If you do cycle on drop handlebars you will need to do some exercises to counterbalance the postural stresses.

Swimming

The buoyancy of water makes swimming one of the few activities which does not involve the joints in any impact. Swimming is an excellent all-round exercise and gives the back muscles good movement. The breast stroke does entail holding the neck and upper back in extension for long periods and you should try to do a length on the back every so often.

Sports and games

You will need to be selective about sporting activities if you have a chronic back disorder. On the whole the benefits of activity must be weighed against a few risks to specific areas of the spine arising from certain sports. Many racket games, such as tennis, squash, and badminton, are one-sided but, performed with due regard for the warnings given on page 70, will do little harm.

With all games involving racket, club, bat, or cue, if the strokes are executed in the correct fashion there is less risk of injury so, whatever your sport, it will pay to develop your technique. There is always the risk of injury to a vulnerable low back from the sudden twist or turn, but the fitter you are and the better your technique the less likely this is to happen.

Golf is a game in which this principle particularly applies. An over-vigorous and uncontrolled swing may place excessive strain on the joints of the lower thoracic spine. The lumbosacral area is more likely to be injured when lifting the ball out of the hole so remember to bend your knees and hips.

Soccer and *rugby* pose different risks for the more youthful spine. If damage or injury to the neck has occurred, you may find heading the ball at soccer leads to some pain, and the rugby scrum may not be a comfortable or safe place to be.

Growing backs should never be placed in the scrum if there is a big difference in size and weight of the participants. Be particularly wary of discomfort in young people with a history of Scheuermann's disease. They may need to play in another position or even try another sport.

Basketball involves a sufficient variety of movement to impose little particular strain on the back other than the unexpected twist or turn. There can be no half measures in a game like this so be sure you are reasonably fit before recommencing it after a lay-off for back injury.

Cricket imposes a variety of stresses on the spine of which the greatest is that of the pace bowler. Ian Botham and Dennis Lillee are two examples of international cricketers who needed spinal surgery because of damage from years of impact to the lower back joints. Pounding down hard pitches and arching the back at the moment of delivery of the ball puts considerable strain on the disc spaces of the lower lumbar joints.

Hockey and *lacrosse*, being one-sided sports, call for a good deal of fitness and flexibility, but do not impose more than mild risk of aggravation to lower back or neck and shoulder regions when playing the long sweep shots.

Limber and loosen

You will minimize the risk of injury with any games you play if you loosen up with a few stretching exercises beforehand. There are probably few sports or games entirely without some risk of potential injury to the back. If you want to play safe you may have to take up chess!

Oriental exercise systems

The exercises from the East are among the oldest systems of movement for health. They have been carefully evolved over several thousand years to achieve total body harmony. They were devised primarily for spiritual development but are gaining popularity in the West for the physical well-being they can impart.

They are all fairly complicated routines which require tuition from an expert, but it is possible to learn some of the simpler sequences from a book.

Yoga

This Indian system of breathing and exercises was evolved to promote *prana*, the life force in the body, as a means to greater spiritual enlightenment. The physical exercises of *hatha yoga* have become popular in the West and most towns have classes run by experienced teachers in adult education institutes or community centres.

Yoga is an excellent way of maintaining the flexibility of the spinal joints and muscles as well as the important guy-rope muscles in the thighs and abdomen. Some of the postures, however, are rather too taxing for backs in which there is joint or disc degeneration. If you have a vulnerable back be very cautious of those involving a shearing or torsional (twisting) stress on the spinal joints. Also, those which are likely to impose pressure on worn joints or narrowed discs must be avoided. These may include the candle, the plough, the forward bend, and the spinal twist. Be guided by a good teacher who will not allow you to go beyond your limits.

The *Salutation to the Sun* is a sequence of yoga postures which is particularly beneficial for maintaining all-round spinal health since it incorporates some of the muscle stretching exercises described earlier.

T'ai chi

This Chinese system of exercise was also developed to mobilize the flow of vital energy (called, by the Chinese, *chi*). It is more valuable for its harmonizing effect and to develop poise and postural balance. The movements are less extreme than those of yoga and are practised widely throughout the Far East where people of all ages can be seen doing their exercises in parks and open spaces each morning.

It is best to have tuition from an expert as the movements need to be done correctly to get the maximum benefit. They are nearly all suitable for the back since the spine is held upright most of the time and there is little danger of pressure on vulnerable joints.

Qi gong

Qi gong (pronounced chee-gung) is another Chinese exercise system in which breathing plays an important role. The rhythmical movements are based on those of animals and birds, such as the crane, and help to develop poise and balance. Like T'ai chi, they can be adapted to people of all ages and abilities.

7. MASSAGE

Getting to grips with back pain

So much of the discomfort of back disorders originates in the soft tissues — the muscles, tendons, and connective tissues — that anything which can keep them pliable and free to function normally will play a major part in the restoration and maintenance of a healthy back. Massage is a direct and immediate way to reduce the spasm, congestion, and fibrous thickening which are often the main source of discomfort in our backs.

The most common component of chronic backache is stiffness. It is particularly prevalent after being in one position for a while, lying down or sitting. The tense muscle fibres have continued to produce their acid wastes and the sluggish blood flow allows these to build up in the area, increasing the congestion in the surrounding connective tissues and making the area more tender.

Sometimes a few fibres within the belly of the muscle become irritated so much that they contract even tighter and form a fibrous knot. This may be not only a source of burning pain, in the back of the shoulders for example, but an irritant to nerve endings which pass messages, via the spinal cord, to other muscle fibres causing secondary spasms. These muscle knots are therefore known as 'trigger points'.

Massage, which you can do at home, is one of the ways of getting to grips with these painful areas. (More specific techniques of neuromuscular work and muscle energy treatments are used by osteopaths, chiropractors, and naturopaths; see Chapter 13.)

Benefits for the back

Massage has benefits at various levels of our bodily functions. There are mechanical, physiological, psychological, and reflex benefits.

Mechanical benefits

* Massage promotes circulation of blood to and from the muscles and connective tissues.
* Massage stimulates drainage of lymph from connective tissues.
* Massage promotes perspiration by increasing circulation.
* Squeezing of muscle tissues creates positive and negative pressures which stimulate the small vessels.
* Massage stretches contracted muscle fibres and loosens congested tissues.

These benefits will be obvious in terms of stiff and painful backs. Arising from these mechanical benefits are some of the known physiological benefits which also enhance them.

Physiological benefits

* Massage increases the release by the brain of hormones, known as endorphins and enkephalins. These are morphine-like substances which reduce pain and inflammation.
* Waste products of muscle activity or inflammation are more rapidly dispersed.
* Negative oxygen balance is corrected.

Psychological benefits

The endorphins and enkephalins also induce a sense of well-being which accounts for some of the psychological benefits of massage. The physical release of muscle spasm reduces tension, and massage is a powerful tool in the reduction of stress.

Reflex benefits

These are based on the long-recognized fact that stimuli applied to one part of the body, may, through nervous connections, influence another part. Massage to tender spots in one part of the back may relieve pain in another part which arises from the secondary spasms described earlier.

Evolution of massage and reflex treatments

Massage is possibly the oldest form of treatment known to man. It must have developed out of the instinctive tendency to rub a sore area or scratch an irritation. As it became evident that this alleviated not only local pains but also more remote areas, the value of manual treatment in relieving many ailments was realized.

The treatment of tender spots led to the discovery of energy centres and reflex zones on the surface which connect with internal systems of the body. The direct benefits of massage were supplemented by the reflex systems of acupressure, shiatsu, and foot zone therapy, which are described later in this chapter.

How to give massage

If yours is the back which is in trouble these instructions are really for someone else, but it is useful for everyone in the family to be familiar with the rudiments of massage.

Lubrication

You will need massage oil. Various oils are available which contain added essences designed to stimulate the circulation or relax the nerves (see page 129). Your health food store will have a selection of these pleasant oils or massage creams. Oil is generally preferable to cream for massage as it spreads much more easily and goes further.

The main purpose of the massage oil is lubrication so a vegetable oil such as sunflower or almond oil will serve just as well.

Position

The subject should lie face downwards on a comfortable surface with a pillow underneath the abdomen or hips. For massage of the neck or shoulders he may sit on a chair or lie face downwards with the head to one side. When you work on the neck, the forehead should rest on a pillow supported by the backs of the hands.

The subject needs to be at a convenient working height for the person giving the massage. If the bed is at the wrong height he could lie on the floor so that you can kneel beside him.

Procedure

There are several essentials to remember when giving a massage:

* the hands need to be warm
* the hands should be relaxed but positive in their actions
* let the hands and fingers mould to the parts you are treating.

Place a little oil in the palm of your hand and spread some on the back or neck, allowing the hand to mould to the body as you do so. Use just enough oil to enable your hands to move over the skin easily. If the subject is hairy you will need rather more but there is no need to put on so much that it runs; you don't need to swim in the stuff!

Massage is given with a variety of movements, the most useful of which are stroking, kneading, and stretching.

Stroking, or gliding, is done with the palms of the hands which are moved upwards on the trunk towards the heart in a steady rhythm. Exert a little more pressure on the upward glide, stroking lightly as you come downwards again.

Kneading may be combined with stroking. The fingers or heel of the hand are used to squeeze and stretch the skin and underlying flesh. Use the thumb and fingers in a gentle pinch and roll manoeuvre on the neck, and the heels of the hands in bigger areas, such as the shoulders and back. When kneading, try to move the skin over the underlying tissues, moving on to each area as you do so. As you become used to using the hands you will be able to feel which strokes are appropriate in each part of the body.

Fig 26 Directions for massage strokes on neck and back

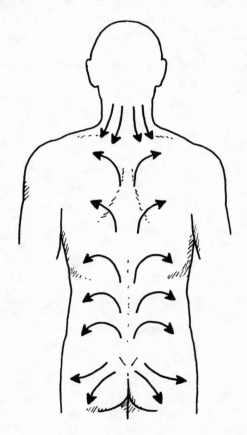

Start with broad moves away from the spine in an upwards and outwards direction, then follow on with smaller circular kneadings in tight or tender areas. On the neck and shoulders you should work downwards in smaller movements from the base of the skull towards the shoulders and upper back. (See Fig 26.)

Knotty spots

As you work over the muscles on either side of the spine you will encounter some areas of hardened contracted fibres. If larger muscles are involved they feel like a piece of rope, over which your fingers or hands jump, instead of the smooth elastic texture of healthy tissues. Where fewer fibres are affected there may be a generally gritty sensation, or more well-defined nodules may be felt. They will all be rather tender, some acutely so.

These are trigger points which can refer pain to other areas of the back or limbs. When you feel these areas of fibrous thickening, work gently over them with the fingers or thumb tips or with the heel of your hand. Move the skin over the underlying tissues with a few repeated strokes, then progress a little to adjacent areas of congestion.

The sensation for the patient should be one of 'hurting that feels good'. The bruised feeling of such trigger points is coupled with a feeling of benefit as the fibres are stretched and released. If there is a more acute sensation, be guided by the tolerance of the subject. Sometimes muscle spasms become so acute, or even inflamed, that they are too sensitive to massage. You must then use hot and cold fomentations to clear the congestion and reduce the inflammation before attempting any other physical procedures.

When to massage the back

Massage is a most comforting and relaxing experience whenever there is acute back pain but it is a valuable preventative of stiffness at other times. In very acute episodes, where vertebral displacements are causing nerve root irritation, you may have to be careful not to involve pressure, which might aggravate pain in the affected area, but general work on the muscles and trigger points, in conjunction with fomentations, will speed up recovery.

The chronic back pain sufferer will invariably have rather stiff muscles which need regular massage so if you or your family become proficient in the simpler strokes you can help each other enormously. For the real resolution of the knottier areas, however, you should have treatment from an experienced masseur or an osteopath who uses the more specific neuromuscular technique in conjunction with correction of the vertebral displacements which are so often responsible for the muscle imbalances.

Massage equipment

For those who do not feel so confident with their hands, various mechanical devices may be used, although none of them have the sensitivity and ability to reach the specific trouble spots that human fingers and thumbs possess.

There are vibratory massagers which are electrically operated and a variety of rollers and pressure devices, some of which are described in Chapter 12.

Reflex therapies

More specific types of massage make use of the reflex connections of one part of the body with another. Special points on the body surface are used to exert an influence on deeper tissues or other areas somewhat removed from the zone of application and also to enhance the functions of the body generally.

The benefits of these techniques — shiatsu, acupressure, and foot and hand reflexology — are less direct than those of normal massage because they act through nervous or energetic connections with the structures they help. They may also encourage the brain to release endorphins.

Acupressure and shiatsu

These are basically similar techniques which treat special points on the body surface.

Acupressure is the stimulation of points which lie along the system of energy channels or meridians used for acupuncture treatment. It is, in fact, an alternative (though less effective) to the needles or heat used by acupuncturists.

Shiatsu — the Japanese system of finger pressure massage — is also applied to acupuncture points but may use other reflex areas. Many other systems of reflex massage are also used. The theory behind the Eastern systems of acupuncture and shiatsu is that the stimulus applied to these points exerts a regulatory effect on the body's energies as they pass along the meridians and connect with organs, such as liver and kidneys which regulate muscle and bone functions. Although these complex theories of energy movement are the only satisfactory explanation for the various effects of acupressure on the different points, it is more likely that the major benefits are local and are induced by the increased output of endorphins by the brain when treatment is given. Other effects may be achieved through nerve reflexes.

You can use acupressure and shiatsu on yourself or your family. It must be regarded as a helpful form of first-aid and supportive treatment in conjunction with other measures to tackle the causes of the pain.

How to apply acupressure

The best tool for treatment is a finger, thumb, or knuckle. Find the point, which will be felt as a slight depression of the flesh in the region indicated by the charts in Fig 27.

Exert a firm but gentle pressure with the tip of the fingers or thumb or use the knuckle of a bent finger for stronger stimulation of more muscular areas. Apply circular kneading movements for one to three minutes, moving the skin over the underlying tissues. Do not rub the fingers over the surface as this will merely irritate the skin.

A slightly bruised sensation or fibrous congestion, as on the trigger points, may be felt but any additional tenderness suggests a need to stop and move on to another point.

The diagram on page 96 shows the most useful points to treat with acupressure or shiatsu if you have acute or chronic

Fig 27 Some acupressure points for back pain

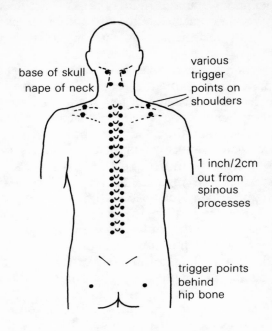

base of skull
nape of neck

various
trigger
points on
shoulders

1 inch/2cm
out from
spinous
processes

trigger points
behind
hip bone

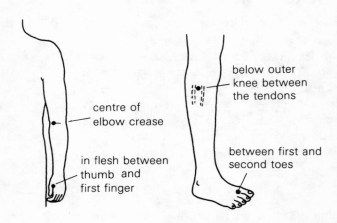

centre of
elbow crease

in flesh between
thumb and
first finger

below outer
knee between
the tendons

between first and
second toes

back pain. Work on points around the painful areas, starting at the top and working downwards.

If the pain is in the neck or shoulders, start with points at the base of the skull and move down to those on either side of the spine and on top of the shoulders.

For the middle and lower back work down from the lower rib points over the lumbar areas. The points on either side of the spine are located about one inch (2–3 cm) from the centre, level with the space between each spinous process. Feel for the natural depression in the flesh but do not be put off by areas of contracted or fibrous tissue. Work on them gently and they will gradually relax.

When you have treated the painful areas finish off with a few minutes' massage of the points on the extremities. Treat the arm points for the upper part of the back and the leg points for the lower half. The points on top of the foot are beneficial for cramp and spasm in any part of the body and should be treated in all cases.

Acupressure and shiatsu points can be treated in conjunction with a general massage.

Foot reflexology

Ancient Egyptian wall paintings depict physicians giving manual treatment to their patients' hands and feet. Several individual parts of the body surface carry an imprint of the whole system. The nose and ears, for example, have acupuncture points which can influence other organs and structures of the body. The hands and feet have particularly accessible reflex zones and these were discovered and utilized by the Egyptian physicians.

The value of the feet as a way to help the whole body was rediscovered and developed in the early 1930s by Eunice Ingham, who was then a masseuse in upper New York State. Later she travelled widely, teaching her system of foot reflexology which she also described in her books *Stories the Feet Can Tell* and *Stories the Feet Have Told* (Ingham Publishing Inc., P.O. Box 12642, St Petersberg, Florida 33733, U.S.A.). Among these stories — all of them true — are many instances of relief to stiff and painful areas in the neck, back, and shoulders, following massage of the foot reflex zones. Eunice Ingham's teaching work is continued by her nephew, Dwight C. Byers, Director of the International Institute of Reflexology.

Fig 28 Foot reflex zones to help the back

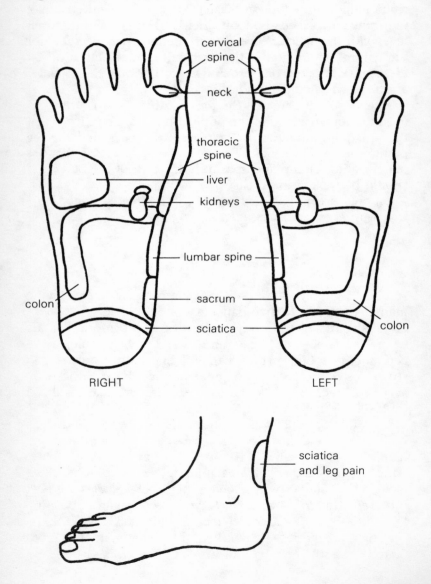

Foot reflexology can be a valuable adjunct to the management of back pain. It is particularly helpful as a prelude to osteopathy or chiropractic, reducing the sensitivity to treatment of the vertebral displacement. It is best applied by a therapist trained by one of the leading organizations (see Appendix) but if you are able to bend your legs sufficiently to reach your feet you may be able to treat some areas yourself. Otherwise ask someone else to do it for you, provided that they have sufficient confidence of touch not to tickle.

How to massage foot reflexes

Most of the important reflex zones are on the sole of the foot so it is best to grasp it with one or both hands over the top and use the fingertips to probe the tender spots underneath.

With the tips of the index or middle fingers exert a firm kneading pressure to the areas indicated in the diagram on page 98. Work on the soft tissues rather than the bones. Treat one organ zone at a time on each foot before moving on to the next, spending no more than two or three minutes on each area. Use broad circular movements moving down the foot from toe to heel on zones such as the neck and spine.

The zone for the spine extends from the big toe to the heel on the inside of each foot. The inside of the lower third of the big toe represents the top of the spinal column, the atlas and axis bones, while the neck zone lies across the joint of the toe with the foot. Other parts of the inner margin of the foot correspond with the rest of the spine. All these areas are represented on both left and right feet.

You may need to work particularly on zones corresponding to the painful part of your back but, because of the important interrelationships of different areas of the spine, you should also massage the rest of the reflex zones. Dwight C. Byers, in his book *Better Health with Foot Reflexology* (Ingham Publishing Inc.), emphasizes the importance of working the spinal areas thoroughly on both feet in every session.

If you find tender areas they may feel rough or gritty and you can knead these gently until the pain diminishes. It may help to place a little oil on the fingers but this will not usually be necessary as they only need to move the skin over the underlying tissues without rubbing the surface too much.

You can work on the feet for five to ten minutes once a day, or more frequently if in pain. Treat the spinal zones, concentrating on the areas which connect to where the pain is, and work on one or two of the other influential organ zones. Important ones are liver and kidney (for their blood purifying effects), lymphatic zones (decongesting), adrenal glands (to encourage steroid production), and colon (to help elimination).

Remember that this is a valuable supportive treatment but that proper attention may be required for the muscles or bony imbalances which are causing the back pain.

Nutrition for the back

A question frequently asked of osteopaths, chiropractors, physiotherapists, and others involved in treatment of the back is 'Does what I eat have anything to do with my back pain?'. Specialists in back problems who take a mainly mechanical view of the spine and its functions often dismiss the idea as nonsense, but modern nutritional biochemistry is producing more and more evidence to show the connection between the food we eat and the health of the muscles, ligaments, and joints.

The quality of our daily food is important, not only for the fabric of the spinal structures, but, through its direct influence in regulating our total well-being, it governs their functions. No matter what mechanical or structural defects may affect us, the functions of the liver, kidneys, stomach, bowels, lungs, and skin will all have a bearing on the way we cope with them. Healthy eating is essential to healthy function of every tissue, particularly those of the back, which must retain resilience, elasticity, and stability.

How food affects your back

Here are just some of the ways in which the fuel we put into our bodies in the form of food and drink influences the function of our backs.

* It provides energy for muscle activity. Inadequate energy leads to weakness and pain in the joints.
* It provides the raw materials to build the connective tissues, muscles, ligaments, and bones. Poor quality material builds poor tissues.
* It provides vitamins, minerals, trace elements, which help to neutralize the waste products of muscle metabolism. Incomplete breakdown and elimination of waste products encourages stagnation in connective tissues with subsequent loss of function and liability to inflammation.

The ability of our bodies to use our nourishment to fulfil these roles depends, of course, on a healthy digestion and food of the right quality.

How diet helps your back

There are three principal ways in which attention to what you are eating, or not eating, can help you with the management of your back pain.

Collagen — the spinal cement

The key to the relationship between nutrition and spinal health is the ground substance, or collagen, which acts as the buffer and packing material between the more definite structures, such as bones and blood vessels.

Collagen acts as the transport medium, conveying nutrients and oxygen from the blood to the muscles and the ligaments. It also transports impurities and acid wastes produced by the muscles in their work so that they can be conveyed by the blood to the bowels and skin for elimination.

It is this dual function of collagen — as an intermediary of nutrition and elimination and as a sort of tissue cement — that makes dietary management such an important tool in the care of the back.

Digestive competence and food intolerance

The digestive enzymes in the mouth, stomach, and duodenum break down the various components of our food into a form which our bodies can use for energy and tissue building, or store for reserves. When these functions are impaired, undigested food may ferment in the intestines or protein molecules may penetrate the gut wall. These molecules are recognized as foreign by the blood cells which produce immune complexes to fight them off.

These complexes may then attack the body's own tissues, especially in the membranes of the joints or the muscle fibres. This gives rise to what are known as auto-immune disorders (the body's defences turning on its own tissues), examples of which are rheumatoid arthritis, and polymyalgia rheumatica.

A similar response is the basis of food intolerance, or so called allergic disorders. Identifying and avoiding the offending foods may help but the basic dysfunction must be corrected if there is to be any long-term improvement.

Quality
You can ensure that the food you use in your basic diet provides the variety and quality which will give you adequate supplies of the raw materials needed for healthy tissues.

Cleansing
It is possible by fasting and controlled diet programmes to assist the body in its cleansing and eliminating functions. Such programmes may fulfil the dual functions of neutralization and removal of the products of oxidation, the free radical compounds. Free radicals are not only damaging to the tissues but may obstruct their uptake of essential nutrients. Such a programme also reduces your exposure to foods of which you may be intolerant.

Reinforcement
The third important aspect of the food factor lies in applied

nutrition — the use of natural nutritional supplements based on the most up-to-date knowledge of nutritional biochemistry to reinforce the functions of your basic foods. The role of specific vitamins, minerals, and trace elements in sustaining healthy connective tissues, in all their forms, is assuming increasing relevance to the management of back pain. Vitamin C is just one such nutrient which has far-reaching possibilities in the treatment of acute and chronic disorders.

Food for a firm foundation

One of the best ways of helping recovery from or preventing back pain is to ensure that your basic diet contains the natural nutrients your body needs. It should provide not only the essential ingredients but be free, as far as possible, from additives and chemical residues, which interfere with the absorption of some nutrients or impose a further toxic burden. Your daily nourishment needs to be *wholefood*.

What is wholefood?

Wholefood has to meet the following criteria:

* grown, where possible, without the use of chemical fertilizers or toxic sprays
* processed and prepared without chemical additives or preservatives, colourants and emulsifiers, etc. (shown on the labels as E-numbers, but some E-numbers represent harmless vegetable dyes)
* served as near to the natural state as possible; cooking should be done only to the degree necessary to make the food palatable.

Biological value

Wholefood is grown and prepared with respect for the environment. It ensures health from the soil upwards, which means that for man, at the top of the food chain, there is the best possible foundation for strong spinal tissues. Unrefined foods have a greater fibre content and provide a higher level of essential nutrients. The biological value — the energy-giving potential — is also greatest in fresh, organically grown raw foods.

Fibre is provided in the diet by vegetables and fruit (especially when eaten raw) and unrefined grains, such as rice, millet, oats, and wheat. Wholemeal bread is a good source. These foods provide the bulk which maintains the muscular functions of the intestines and prevents constipation. They also act as a base for the intestinal bacteria which help to make certain vitamins available to us.

Bran, used by many people for its fibre content, binds certain trace elements, such as iron and zinc, making them unavailable to the body, so it should not be used as the only source of fibre in the diet.

Food which may pose problems

There are some foods in the everyday diet of many people which may pose problems. They undermine the health over many months and years by 'filling without feeding', by burdening the body tissues with toxic compounds, and by disrupting the energy-producing and immunity-building processes.

They are really non-foods because we can manage perfectly well without them. Nevertheless, in moderation they may add variety and interest to our diet, although there are often more nutritious and palatable alternatives.

These non-foods are the *red-flag foods* — to be approached with caution, and only if you really have to.

Sugar and sweeteners

Sugar is ubiquitous in the modern diet and as a consequence most people consume too much. Apart from direct consumption in drinks and on food, sugar is an ingredient of things such as bread, biscuits, tinned and packaged savouries, sauces, dressings, and desserts. In nearly all its forms — glucose, treacle, syrups, even processed honey — sugar is highly concentrated and absorbed too quickly. This may give quick energy but it is not lasting energy and repeated rapid absorption disrupts the metabolism leading to problems of immunity, intolerances, muscle aches, and joint pains.

The pattern of excessive sugar consumption (especially with caffeine in coffee, and cigarettes) can lead to a condition of chronic low blood sugar (rapid absorption of sugar overstimulates the secretion of insulin, the sugar-digesting hormone, which leaves the energy levels low). According to Martin L. Budd, N.D., author of *Low Blood Sugar* (Thorsons, 1984) this situation causes over-acidity in the stomach, poor calcium absorption, and reduction of blood calcium levels.

Low calcium levels may result in nerve irritability, muscular cramps and spasms, and a reduction of bone calcium as it is leached out to try and meet the demands of the other tissues. It is better to derive our sweetness from fresh or dried fruits.

Artificial sweeteners are not recommended as their cumulative toxic effect cannot be ruled out.

White flour and refined grains

Many basic grain foods, such as wheat, rice, and barley, have had the outer layer and germ removed in the milling process. With these are lost the most nutritious parts containing essential vitamins such as those of the B complex, minerals such as calcium, and trace elements such as zinc and chromium.

Regular consumption of white flour produce and other refined cereal grains may, therefore, lead to a deficiency of the nutrients which protect the spine and the nervous system. Because much of the natural fibre is lost in the refining process these products may also contribute to constipation.

Consumption of unrefined grains — wholemeal flour, brown rice — may not entirely guarantee adequate nourishment because modern farming methods, using pesticides and fertilizers to increase yields, are causing soils to become deficient in essential elements, such as manganese and selenium. Organically farmed produce should be chosen where possible.

Salt

Salt is another widely occurring substance in food. Salt is added to many processed, tinned, and packaged foods apart from its use at the table. Excessive sodium disrupts the fluid metabolism, causing water to move into the intercellular spaces. It also disturbs the mineral balance in the blood, creating problems with the levels of potassium and magnesium.

The old idea that salt is needed to prevent cramp is not strictly accurate. Muscle cramps occur when there is a disturbance in the ratio of sodium to potassium and it may often be preferable to supplement the latter rather than salt.

Table salt is too concentrated and unbalances the body fluids. Sodium occurring naturally in vegetables is in a form balanced by the potassium content so it causes no problems.

Tea and coffee

The principal problem ingredient of tea and coffee is caffeine which, among other things, may cause restless legs in bed and insomnia with nervousness. Tea contains about 50mg per cup of caffeine and coffee 100mg per cup and, for some people quite low levels of caffeine can interfere with the absorption of vitamins and minerals.

According to Dr Stephen Davies and Dr Alan Stewart, authors of *Nutritional Medicine* (Pan, 1987), consumption of these beverages reduces iron absorption to about one third of the normal intake. Iron is important to the oxygen-carrying capacity of the blood, so regular tea and coffee consumption may contribute to the deterioration of the connective tissues in the spine.

Alcohol

Beer, wines, and spirits interfere with absorption of most vitamins — especially those of the B complex and vitamin C — and some minerals. Enjoy them in moderation for social occasions but recognize the negative effects.

Alcohol is absolutely taboo in any case of acute back pain. The price of relaxation, or any anaesthetic effects of a few stiff drinks, will be further fuelling of the inflammation.

A cumulative effect

The actual harm these red-flag foods can do will vary enormously from person to person. Some people with a good constitution, or who are basically well-nourished, can consume them regularly without apparent ill-effects; others may find that even small quantities of some trouble-makers upset them and trigger off the aches and pains.

The best policy is to exclude these substances from your basic menu but not to worry if they crop up when dining out or on special occasions. The damage is usually only cumulative over a long period and the healthily functioning body can neutralize and eliminate the free radical compounds they invariably contain. It is, however, wise to be especially careful to avoid such poisons when you have any acute pain or inflammation in the spinal joints.

A guide to healthy eating

The suggestions given here are based on the general principles of a wholefood diet adequate to maintain good health, low in fats, refined carbohydrates, and salt, and virtually free of the items which are likely to burden your body or deprive the back of its essential nutrients.

A number of alternatives are given for each meal so that you can select to suit your tastes and provide variety to the week. If you are not accustomed to this type of food don't be too daunted. Introduce these measures a little at a time, perhaps by changing the pattern of one meal, such as breakfast, for a week or two, before tackling the others.

Basic health diet

Daily menu

On rising   Cider vinegar or lemon juice drink: one dessertspoonful in a cup of warm water with half a teaspoonful of honey if necessary. Fresh fruit juice or a herb tea may be used as an alternative.

Is your breakfast giving you backache?

The typical breakfast fare of tea or coffee, cereal, and toast could be a recipe for back pain. The ingredients of this important first meal of the day are either so lacking in nourishment or so likely to rob nutrients from other foods, that they may make breakfast a dangerous meal. Those who skip it and make time for only a cup of tea or coffee are loading the dice even more heavily against themselves.

Consider what most people push down their throats before rushing to the office or factory: they start with tea or coffee, maybe two or three cups, laced with sugar. If they take them with milk any nourishment this provides is likely to be cancelled out by the caffeine in the tea or coffee, and the calcium will almost certainly be stolen by the sugar, so it won't be available to the body.

Next comes cereal, usually made from highly refined grains, with much of the nourishment removed. The manufacturers do put in a few synthetic and biologically inferior minerals and vitamins, but even they will stand little chance of getting to where they are needed in the onslaught of caffeine. Toast is white, deficient in the B vitamins and spread with salty butter or margarine and sugary marmalade, creating further mineral imbalances.

These are washed down with more tea or coffee and possibly rounded off with a cigarette, which robs the vital vitamin C.

That is what many people might call a 'good breakfast'. An alarmingly large number of people make do with just a hasty coffee, and little else, but their spines cannot 'make do' with the chronic lack of nutrients and, over the months and years, may deteriorate to the point of breakdown.

Make sure that your breakfast isn't giving you backache.

Breakfast	One of the following may be taken: fresh fruit in season, dried fruit (e.g. apricots, prunes) baked or puréed apple with raisins, muesli, wholemeal or rye bread toasted or fresh, with unsalted butter or sunflower margarine and honey, pure fruit jam, or savoury spread. If a drink is required, a glass of pure unsweetened fruit juice, China or herb tea, coffee substitute, or hot savoury drink (e.g. yeast extract) may be taken.
Mid-morning	If a drink is required, take mineral water, fruit juice, herb tea, or coffee substitute. If a snack is required use a wholemeal biscuit or a little fruit, nuts, or sunflower seeds.
Lunch	Mixed vegetable salad, containing a selection of raw vegetables in season, with a baked jacket potato and/or baked onion, and cheese or milled nuts. Salad dressing of vegetable oil with lemon juice or cider vinegar. Wholemeal or rye bread or biscuits with savoury spread. *or* Warm savoury dish (egg, lean meat, fish, cheese, nut, tofu, or other savoury) with conservatively cooked vegetables and baked jacket potato, or cereal grains (rice, couscous, millet). For dessert — soaked dried fruit, baked apple, fresh fruit, muesli, yogurt, carrageen or natural fruit jelly.
Mid-afternoon	As mid-morning.
Evening meal	Alternative to lunch. The salad meal may be taken at midday or in the evening according to preference and convenience. It is desirable to have one raw salad meal per day throughout the year. Dessert — as for lunch.
On retiring	As for mid-morning.

Dietary detoxifying

The waste products of energy production and muscular work have to be disposed of. The skin, lungs, bowels, and kidneys generally take most of these out of the body but they sometimes accumulate more rapidly than they can be eliminated and become deposited in the tissues. The connective tissues are a favoured site of storage for these toxic deposits.

These waste products, together with those derived from materials taken into the body as additives, pesticides, and other environmental poisons, form compounds in the body known as free radicals. Free radicals have the effect of oxidizing tissues in the body, thereby damaging the cells and creating inflammation.

Dietary programmes designed to rest the body physiology not only reduce the intake of harmful compounds but actually allow the eliminative functions to catch up, reducing the encumbrance in the tissues and healing areas of inflammation. The basic wholefood diet will provide a mild detoxification, by virtue of its relative freedom from free radicals and abundance of antioxidant nutrients, but the most effective cleansing procedure is the fast. Diets of varying stringency between these two extremes are possible. All are simple to follow at home and they are valuable tools in dealing with acute and chronic back pain.

If you have acute pain with inflammation of nerve roots and surrounding tissues a short fast in conjunction with bed rest and fomentations will help to speed up recovery. With the more chronic aches and pains the cleansing diet programme will be worth trying.

These approaches have a proven value in the treatment of arthritis and rheumatism. The late Giraud W. Campbell, an American osteopath, was able to demonstrate, by before and after X-ray films, a reduction of degenerative changes in arthritic joints following the application of a seven-day detoxification programme described in his book *A Doctor's Proven New Home Cure for Arthritis* (Thorsons, 1989).

The programme described here provides a short-term cleansing routine to assist in the treatment of acute pain, and a slightly longer routine for the treatment of chronic rheumatism and arthritic conditions of the spine. This may also be used as a prelude to, or extension of, the short-term diet.

The alkaline anti-inflammatory diet (AAID)

This programme commences with a short fast moving on to a diet of alkaline foods which counteract the tissue acidity present in many rheumatic and inflammatory conditions.

Use the AAID whenever there is acute neck or back pain or severe sciatica. These pains are often due to irritation of nerve roots near the spine and the dietary approach will support your efforts with compresses and gentle massage to clear the congestion.

Day 1

On rising	One glass of hot water with the juice of half a lemon or one dessertspoonful of lemon juice or apple cider vinegar.
Breakfast	One large tumbler of freshly expressed juice of apple, grape, carrot, orange, or pineapple. These may be diluted with a little mineral water. Canned or bottled juices may be used but must be pure, unsweetened, and free from preservatives or other additives. (If using pineapple juice dilute it by half with mineral water).
Mid-morning	One glass of mineral water with a slice of lemon.
Lunch	Pure juice as for breakfast. You may combine two juices, such as carrot and apple, or orange and pineapple.
Mid-afternoon	One glass of mineral water with a slice of lemon.
Evening	Pure juices either singly or combined as for lunch.
On retiring	Warm water with one teaspoonful of vegetable concentrate, yeast extract or concentrated apple juice.

Day 2
The alkaline saturation of your system is continued by staying entirely on fresh raw fruit. Choose from the following list according to availability: apples, pears, grapes, melons, peaches, pineapples.

Citrus fruits (oranges, grapefruits, lemons), tomatoes, gooseberries, and plums have been excluded as some people react to them with joint and muscle aches. The citrus juices on the first day may not impose the same problems. Bananas are too starchy for this early stage of cleansing.

Eat enough to satisfy the appetite at each meal. Between meals use mineral water or fruit juices or warm drinks as for Day 1.

Day 3

On rising	Fruit juice or hot cider vinegar and honey drink.
Breakfast	Fresh fruit as before. This may be taken as a fruit salad with a handful of sunflower or pumpkin seeds.
Mid-morning	Juice or herb tea.
Lunch	Mixed raw salad prepared according to basic health diet (see page 108).
Afternoon	Juice or herb tea.
Evening meal	Mixed raw salad again or mixed vegetable stew or broth. (See recipe, page 114.)
On retiring	Savoury or juice drink.

Cleansing diet for chronic aches

The following two-week programme provides a 'spring clean' regimen for people with chronic backache and muscular rheumatism or arthritis. It combines the initial alkaline diet with a follow-up programme free of the foods likely to cause further tissue acidity but rich in antioxidant compounds. This will provide a balanced programme for most people with allergy or intolerance problems.

Days 1–3
Commence the treatment with three days on fresh fruit and/or vegetable juices only. (Try 24 hours on juices and two days

A mineral-rich stew

Fresh vegetables are the richest source of many minerals and vitamins essential for strong healthy spinal tissues. These nutrients are often leached out in cooking and thrown away with the water. This recipe enables you to use a rich variety of health-giving vegetables in an easily digestible form without throwing away the essential minerals.

Ingredients
Two large potatoes, chopped into approximately half inch (1 cm) pieces; 6 oz (170g/1 cup) carrots shredded or sliced; 6 oz beetroot shredded and sliced; 6 oz celery, leaves and all, chopped into half inch pieces; 6 oz of any other available vegetables — beetroot tops, turnips, turnip tops, parsley, cabbage, or a little of everything.

Method
Use stainless steel, enamelled, or earthenware utensils. Fill the utensils with 3 pints (1.7 litres) of water and slice the vegetables directly into the water to prevent oxidation. Cover and cook slowly for at least half an hour. Let stand for another half hour, cool until warm and serve. If not used immediately, keep in the refrigerator. Warm up before serving. Can be used without straining as a stew.

on fruit.) If on juices, take one tumblerful 4–5 times per day. You may take as much as your appetite demands of fresh fruit. Any kind of fresh fruit except rhubarb and bananas may be taken. If you have rheumatism, arthritis or skin problems you should also avoid citrus fruit. No sugar, either white or brown, is to be used for sweetening. If any fruit cannot be eaten without sweetening, omit it.

Drinks during these first three days should consist of pure unsweetened fruit or vegetable juices, e.g. apple, grape, (orange), pineapple (dilute 50 per cent). If a warm drink is required you may have one teaspoonful of vegetable extract (available from a health food store) dissolved in a cup of hot water. Mineral water or plain water is permissible.

Days 4–7

Breakfast   Drink of fruit juice. Fresh fruit as desired or baked apple with raisins.

Between meals Herb teas, fruit juice, or savoury extract in warm water.

Lunch   Raw salad and dressing (see Basic Health Diet, page 110). As a dessert use fresh fruit only, cut up into fruit salad sprinkled with wheat germ or milled nuts, and moistened with unsweetened pineapple or grape juice if desired.

Evening meal   Raw salad again and dressing, or vegetable broth flavoured with vegetable or yeast extract. For dessert, use fresh fruit or baked or stewed apple or soaked dried prunes or apricots.

Second week

Breakfast   Fresh fruit or baked or stewed apple or dried fruit (e.g. raisins, apricots, prunes). Nuts if desired with the fruit. A fruit salad may be made with wheat germ or grated nuts sprinkled over it and a syrup of honey and water to flavour.

Between meals Herb tea, savoury drink, or fruit juice. Juices may be also be taken as an aperitif to main meals.

Lunch   Raw salad as before or the midday meal and evening meal may be transposed. Raisins or sultanas or a few whole or grated nuts may be added to the salad to give variety. You may also have one or two slices of brown rye bread or rye biscuits with a scraping of butter and a small portion of low fat cheese with the salad. Alternatively, a baked jacket potato, with a little sunflower seed oil. Fresh fruit as dessert.

Evening meal   Two or three conservatively cooked vegetables. Light savoury dish made with eggs, low fat cheese, nuts, tofu, or cereal grains (e.g. brown rice, millet, buckwheat, or rye). Steamed fish may be used as an alternative, or vegetable broth or stew. Fresh fruit as dessert.

Are supplements necessary?

There are many nutrients essential to protect and heal connective tissues and most of these, it may be argued, should be provided in our basic diet. The wholefood diet is certainly richer in vitamins, minerals, and trace elements but under conditions of stress such as you may endure with backache the demand for certain vitamins and minerals is greater than the food can provide.

Sometimes digestive efficiency may also be impaired for a variety of reasons. Certain illnesses which have made extra demands on the immune system may leave the stomach, liver, and spleen less efficient in their functions of processing and distributing nourishment to the body; it will be necessary to use good quality supplements prepared with natural ingredients in the context of a good basic diet and lifestyle. You cannot expect to get the maximum benefit from regular supplements of vitamin C if, for example, you are still smoking twenty cigarettes a day.

Minerals and trace elements

Minerals are the basic chemicals of life. They form a major part of the structure of bones and connective tissues as well as fulfilling important roles in the biochemical changes which enable us to produce energy for muscle function and to transmit the nerve messages which motivate our movements.

Mineral supplements

Minerals are active in our bodies in a compound form. A positive ion (cation) unites with a negative ion (anion); for example, the cation magnesium combines with the anion phosphorus to form magnesium phosphate. In this form they are carried to the cell membrane where it can absorb its requirements selectively.

Some authorities believe that more active absorption from the intestines, and by the individual cells of the body, is possible when the mineral is combined with an organic compound, such as orotic acid, or an amino acid chelate (chelation is the process of binding of a mineral to a protein compound). You will find most mineral supplements are now sold as the orotate or the chelate which is a good form to ensure absorption, though many naturopaths prefer the physiologically less crude approach of the Celloid formulations, in which the mineral compounds are prescribed in physiological doses according to the patient's individual health indications.

Choosing supplements

So many supplements are now sold, either singly or in compounds, and the choice may seem a nightmare. Be guided by your health food store proprietor who will usually stock the best brands. Health food stores may also have combined vitamin, mineral, and herbal formulations.

Dosage of mineral supplements

Unless specifically recommended, dosage will vary according to the strength and form in which a particular mineral is available. Be guided by the manufacturer's recommendations unless more specific figures are given in the descriptions which follow.

Important minerals for the back

Calcium

Most of the body's calcium is found in bones and teeth but it is also involved in other biochemical reactions concerning the muscles and nerves. Blood calcium levels are regulated by the parathyroid glands, two small glands beside the thyroid gland in the neck. When there is insufficient calcium absorbed from our diet these glands will encourage its removal from the bones. A consequence of this may be joint pains and arthritis with the long-term likelihood of osteoporosis.

Inactivity or lack of stress to the bones increases their calcium loss. Astronauts experiencing weightlessness showed significant losses of calcium. If you need to rest with back pain it is important to get back on your feet as soon as possible.

Sources: legumes, green leafy vegetables, broccoli, nuts, seeds, soya milk, and egg shells! (Dr Carl Pfeiffer, in his book *Mental and Elemental Nutrients* (Keats Publishing, 1975), suggests standing an egg in cider vinegar for 24 hours to soften the shell and then using the whole egg, with shell, in a blender to make an egg nog.)

Synergists: magnesium, zinc, phosphorus.

Supplements: calcium orotate or gluconate, or amino chelate. Also present in Dolomite tablets (with magnesium), but ensure that this is a brand free of any toxic metals. Bonemeal is an alternative source of calcium for non-vegetarians. Calcium needs efficient stomach acids for adequate absorption; too little or too much acid can impair uptake.

Magnesium

Magnesium is closely linked with calcium in body chemistry, particularly in the movement of minerals in and out of cells. Magnesium is necessary for energy production, nerve transmission, and muscle contractions. Refined grains, refined sugars, and fat are low in magnesium. It is easily lost in cooking, and its absorption is blocked by the oxalic acid in spinach and rhubarb, and the phytic acid in bran. When magnesium is low in the serum, muscle cramps and tremors are more likely. Magnesium also enhances the absorption of calcium from food and prevents its loss from the body.

Sources: nuts, seafoods, soyabeans, grains, green leafy vegetables (in which it is a component of chlorophyll), and hard water.

Synergists: vitamins B1, B6, calcium. The calcium to magnesium ratio should be 2:1 in the body. (Cows' milk is low in magnesium and high in calcium so children who take a lot of milk may become deficient in magnesium.)

Supplements: magnesium orotate, magnesium amino chelate.

Phosphorus

Phosphorus is also involved in the formation of bones and teeth but is abundant in the diet, so it does not usually need supplementing. In fact, excessive phosphorus may increase the need for calcium and magnesium.

Sources: milk, nuts, wholegrain cereals, eggs, meat, fish, legumes.

Potassium

Potassium is essential for correct function of muscles and the nervous system. A deficiency may result in muscle fatigue, cramps, and nervous sensitivity, and can be induced by drugs such as aspirin, diuretics, steroids, and laxatives. Sodium and potassium are closely linked in our physiology and too much salt in the diet can disturb the ratio of these minerals towards potassium deficiency. Potassium is found plentifully in vegetables, fruit, and wholegrains but supplements may be needed if you are particularly sensitive to nerve pains of a sharp shooting nature. They are also necessary for people who are taking, or who have taken, large amounts of pain-killers, diuretics, or steroids.

Sources: fruit (especially grapes), vegetables, root vegetables (save and use the liquid in which they are cooked), wheatgerm, lentils, nuts.

Synergists: magnesium, sodium.

Supplements: a physiologically balanced compound of potassium, such as the Celloid formulation used by some practitioners, is preferable. It is also available as the orotate and chelate supplemental form.

Trace elements

These are mineral compounds used by the body in very small but significant amounts. Nutrients such as iron, zinc, copper, and manganese are classed as trace elements. Their importance to the body structure and function is only gradually becoming evident, but does seem to be most significant in the case of a number of them.

Zinc and copper, for example, are needed for the formation of elastic fibres in muscles and connective tissues. If these elements are deficient there can be overstretching of the tissues causing the stretch marks which can be seen across the lower back in some people. These can be regarded as a sign of poor supporting ability of the collagen tissue.

Healthy connective tissues also contain high levels of silicon, and Dr S. Davies and Dr A. Stewart, authors of *Nutritional Medicine*, have observed that certain sufferers from joint disorders have lower levels of manganese, suggesting that this element plays an important role in protecting the joint surface. This may link to its role in activating enzymes necessary for the utilization of vitamins C and B.

Many of the trace elements are lost from our food by processing but a wholefood diet will usually provide all that we need. If antagonists, such as tea, coffee, alcohol, or sugar, have been consumed in any quantity it may be necessary to supplement the normal diet. Then it is important to get a correct balance, and although individual trace elements may be recommended by a naturopath, a multi-mineral compound from natural souces available from health food stores would be better for self-prescribing.

Vitamins

As with minerals, the body's demand for certain vitamins when under physical or emotional stress is considerable, and possibly well beyond that provided by a good modern diet.

For basic back maintenance, however, an abundance of the foods rich in the relevant vitamins should provide adequate nourishment.

Vitamin A

Because this vitamin is concerned with the stability of cell membranes it may have some protective role for the joint linings, reducing the likelihood of inflammation. The vitamin A precursor, *beta carotene*, has an antioxidant effect and it is also a valuable protective nutrient against free radical damage.

Sources: fish, liver, kidneys, eggs, carrots, cabbage, oranges, and other yellow fruits.

Synergists: best used with vitamin E, vitamin C, and selenium (a trace element).

Supplements: vitamin A can be toxic in high doses taken over several months, but up to 10,000IU daily may be taken by most adults with complete safety.

Vitamin B

There are a number of B vitamins, all interrelated, but of varying importance to the sufferer from back troubles. Vitamin B6 (pyridoxine), for example, is essential for the manufacture of collagen and elastin fibrils (the small fibres in muscles). Vitamin B5 (pantothenic acid) is concerned with muscle coordination and is reported to be of benefit for arthritis of the joints.

Other vitamins of the B complex play vital roles in the function of nerves, reducing sensitivity and susceptibilty to pain, as well as playing a role in anti-inflammatory mechanisms.

Since most of the B vitamins are synergistic, or dependent upon each other, it is better to use a B complex formulation for supplementing, and this is advisable anyway if taking a single B vitamin, such as B6 (which also needs zinc for its proper absorption).

Sources: liver, organ meats, whole grains, brewer's yeast, eggs, green leafy vegetables.

Supplements: brewer's yeast, B complex preparations (hypoallergenic formulations are best).

Vitamin C

Vitamin C plays a major role in a wide variety of bodily functions and it features strongly in the nutritional requirements of the spine, both structurally and functionally. The connective tissues require vitamin C to retain elasticity and strength, possibly because of its oxygen-sparing effects. Vitamin C is necessary for us to utilize amino acids, the building blocks of protein. When vitamin C becomes deficient ligaments and muscles weaken and important minerals are lost.

Vitamin C levels vary according to the amount of stress, muscle activity, and infection or injury. It helps us to combat inflammation and it protects the joint surfaces against auto-immune disorders such as rheumatoid arthritis. Vitamin C is also reduced by smoking; studies suggest that heavy smokers are slower in recovering from back pain.

Dr James Greenwood Jr, Clinical Professor of Neurosurgery at Baylor University College of Medicine, found that a significant number of his patients with early disc lesions were able to avoid surgery when prescribed vitamin C supplements when compared with those who did not take them. Furthermore, he found a reduced rate of recurrence of problems among cases who had undergone surgery when they were prescribed vitamin C.

Sources: fruits, green leafy vegetables, broccoli, sprouts, cauliflower, liver, potatoes, green peppers.

Supplements: should be taken in a combined form with bioflavonoids (vitamin P), with which the C is found in nature. Half to one gram per day, or more, may be taken (but caution with long-term administration if you have a history of kidney stones or if you are on low-dose contraceptive pill — seek naturopathic advice).

Wonder foods

Some of the foods you can obtain from your health food store have gained a special reputation for their benefits in conditions of the muscles and joints. They may give an added boost to your nutritional programme for the management of back pain.

Brewer's yeast: is a valuable source of vitamins of the B complex and also has some reputation for encouraging the production of oestrogen, which prevents osteoporosis.

Apple cider vinegar: is famous for its beneficial effects in alleviating arthritis. One dessertspoonful in a glass of warm water before meals may help to improve stomach acid function and assist calcium absorption.

Cod liver oil: is a valuable source of vitamin D, necessary for calcium metabolism, and of polyunsaturated fats.

Linseed oil: one to two dessertspoonsful daily provide an excellent source of polyunsaturated fatty acids, which are precursors of the anti-inflammatory prostaglandins.

Green-lipped mussel: this extract of a New Zealand shellfish has proved beneficial in some forms of arthritis, possibly because of its rich source and unique balance of essential minerals.

Vitamin D

This vitamin is best known for its role in improving the absorption and assimilation of calcium. Vitamin D is formed by the action of sunlight on the skin but also occurs in certain foods.

The dietary intake may need supplementing in the elderly and those exposed to very little sunlight. Supplements are usually combined with vitamin A and it should only be taken as part of a compound formulation.

Sources: fish liver oils, eggs, cheese.

9. BACK TO NATURE

Herbal and homoeopathic help

Back pain doesn't always come and go to order and coping with the stiffness and discomfort during a busy working day, when it is not possible to rest or apply fomentations, can be difficult. The multi-million pound industry in pain-killing drugs has been fuelled substantially by the search for quick relief of back pain. Even those who recognize that they may be masking the real causes have, at times, reluctantly resorted to them.

Nature, however, has rich resources — age-old plant and mineral substances which can often give remarkable relief from back pain by actually promoting the body's own healing processes, rather than merely blocking the pain messages. Herbal and homoeopathic medicines act differently from pain-killing drugs and are, therefore, less immediate in their effect but their benefits are likely to be more lasting.

They are certainly more suited to individual needs than the universal aspirin. They act in a variety of ways according to the properties of the plant. Some will encourage circulation and drainage, aiding dispersal of waste products. Others will reduce muscle stiffness, and yet others will nourish and strengthen weakened tissues. They need to be selected carefully, therefore, to meet your particular needs, and, beyond the first-aid repertory given here, you would be greatly helped by the expertise of a qualified medical herbalist or homoeopath.

Some herbal and homoeopathic remedies need to be used for a number of weeks or months and may safely be taken in this way to alleviate chronic rheumatic or arthritic tendencies, or to strengthen weakened tissues. Others, especially homoeopathic medicines, can be used for a short period to give more immediate relief. Generally herbal medicines are beneficial for chronic back problems whilst homoeopathic remedies are more convenient and effective for the acute episodes. Most preparations can be conveniently taken throughout the day, so they are a way of getting nature to your back when it is being difficult.

Herbal medicines

There is a tradition of plant medicines in every part of the world and so there is a tremendous range of preparations which can be used in a wide variety of ways. Although different regions have their favourite indigenous plants, there are some which enjoy universal fame for their special properties as healing aids in musculoskeletal conditions.

Medicinal herbs are not only used orally as tablets, dried plants, infusions and decoctions, but may be added to baths, or applied as poultices, plasters, and liniments. They may be used singly or in combinations of two or more ingredients.

Medicines by mouth

Herbs may be prepared in several ways for administration by mouth. The easiest form for use is the infusion.

An *infusion* is prepared from the fresh plant or the dried herb. If you have access to the fresh plant in your own garden this is an ideal form to use but most of the plants recommended here may be available as dried herbs from a herbal supplier or health food store. Some herbs may be available in tablet or liquid form ready for immediate use.

Preparing an infusion

Use a pestle and mortar to gently crush the fresh plant or grind the dried herb to the consistency of tea or tobacco. You will need about 1oz (30g) of dried herb, or just under 3oz (80g) of the fresh herb, to 1 pint (500ml) of water. Pour boiling water over the herbs then cover the vessel and keep in a warm place to steep for ten to fifteen minutes, stirring occasionally. Then strain and use the liquid in teacupful doses two to three times daily.

Another method is to use one teaspoonful of the dried herb in a cup of hot water.

Herbs for back disorders

Black cohosh (*Cimicifuga racemosa*). The root is used as a blood cleanser for muscular rheumatism and rheumatoid arthritis.

Bogbean (*Menyanthes trifoliata*). The plant is used as a tonic herb for rheumatic tendencies.

Celery (*Apium graveolens*). The seed is used as a tonic, diuretic (increases the kidney and bladder function), cleansing in rheumatic disorders.

Meadowsweet (*Spiraea ulmaria*). The plant is used for muscle and joint pains, and as a tonic to mucous membranes.

Golden seal (*Hydrastis canadensis*). The root is used as a blood cleanser, and tonic to membranes; it helps other herbs to diffuse.

Wild yam (*Dioscorea villosa*). The root is used. It is anti-inflammatory, anti-spasmodic, and relaxes nervous irritation. It is also used for muscular rheumatism.

Passion flower (*Passiflora incarnata*). The plant is used as a nerve relaxant for spasms and neuralgias.

Crampbark (*Viburnum opulus*). The bark is used as an anti-spasmodic to the muscles, and a nerve relaxant.

Devil's claw (*Harpagophytum procumbens*). The plant is used for rheumatism and arthritis.

Yarrow (*Achillea millefolium*). The plant is used as a gentle stimulant. It opens pores and purifies the blood, and is good for stiffness in muscles due to cold damp weather.

Poke root (*Phytolacca decandra*). The root and berries are used as a stimulating cleanser for muscle congestion, and are good for chronic muscular stiffness.

These herbs are best used in combinations, selecting them according to the type of back pain you have. For stiff muscles with intermittent joint pain, use black cohosh, bogbean, celery, poke root, and golden seal in equal parts.

For more acute conditions, with spasm and inflammation, combine crampbark, golden seal, meadowsweet, passion flower, wild yam, and yarrow in equal parts. Increase the proportion of passion flower if there is difficulty in sleeping because of pain.

Herbal baths

Dried or fresh herbs may be added to a hot bath. The physical benefits of the heat are supplemented by the medicinal properties of the plants which diffuse through the skin.

The herbs can be placed in a cheesecloth or muslin bag and immersed in the water like a tea bag, or the bag can be hung from the hot tap as the water runs into the bath. Ready-made infusions may also be added to the bath.

Plants can be selected for their stimulating effects, or as relaxants where there is congestion and stiffness. Use a combination of some of the following tonic and stimulating herbs: basil (*Ocinum basilicum*), bay (*Laurus nobilis*), fennel (*Foeniculum vulgare*), lavender (*Lavendula spica*), pine (*Pinus sylvestris*), rosemary (*Rosemarinus officinalis*), and thyme (*Thymus vulgaris*).

Relaxing herbs include chamomile (*Matricaria recutita*), and lime flowers (*Tilia europaea*).

Moor extract baths

The moors of many parts of Europe yield a peat which has been used for generations in the treatment of muscular and rheumatic disorders. The therapeutic properties of the vegetation, compressed through many hundreds of years, appear to have been concentrated and preserved. Liquid or powdered moor extracts are sometimes available from health food stores and herbal suppliers.

Poultices and plasters

For a back which is sore and sensitive to the touch, herbal poultices can be most comforting. The bruised leaf or root of the plant may be applied direct or between gauze. The latter method is preferable for some plants, such as comfrey leaves, which are rather hairy and would irritate if applied direct.

The herbs may also be applied in the form of a paste. The crushed fresh plants or dried herbs are mixed with a little hot water and added to a paste prepared from flour, bran, or cornmeal. *The Encyclopaedia of Herbs and Herbalism*, edited by Dr Malcolm Stewart (Orbis, 1979), suggests 60g (2oz) of dried herbs with 500ml (17fl oz) of loose paste. The paste is sandwiched between thin cloth and applied to the skin.

Medical herbalists may also prepare plasters using a wax base. The plaster adheres to the skin with the help of body heat. On the Continent it was common practice to apply plasters containing stimulating compounds such as cayenne pepper, ginger, or cantharidin, a counter-irritant prepared from the bodies of ants which yield formic acid.

Herbs which may be used for poultices include pepper (*Capsicum minimum*), ginger (*Zingiber officinalis*), lobelia (*Lobelia inflata*), and comfrey (*Symphytum officinalis*) — the first three for strains and stiffness of muscles and ligaments in the back, and the comfrey for deeper aches in the bones.

Liniments and massage oils

These are mixtures of the herbs with alcohol or cider vinegar, or vegetable oil, which can be used for massage. The herbal ingredients are generally stimulating but may be relaxing and cooling for inflamed surfaces.

The American herbalist, Jethro Kloss, in his classic book *Back to Eden* (Longview Publishing, 1939), suggests boiling one tablespoonful of cayenne pepper in one pint (560ml) of cider vinegar for ten minutes. This makes a powerful stimulating application for deep congestion and strains.

Olbas oil is a mixture of aromatic and stimulating plant oils, such as wintergreen and eucalyptus. It is of value for acute generalized pain in the spine and muscles. Apply it and work it in gently.

Various liniments and oils for massage are available from health food stores and some chemists.

Aromatherapy oils are combinations of essential oils selected for their properties of relaxing, toning, or stimulating the spinal tissues. Some formulations are available from health food stores and chemists. A large quantity of the raw ingredients — flowers, leaves, seeds, or barks — are needed to prepare the essential oils, so they are expensive, but a little goes a long way. Only a few drops need to be added to a massage oil or to a hot bath. These oils can be powerful, so it is important not to use more than the recommended quantities.

Ointments and creams

Ointments and creams enable the medicinal substance to remain in continuous contact with the affected part. The base is generally beeswax or lanolin to which the infused oil of the plant is added.

Arnica cream, available from health food stores and homoeopathic pharmacies, is beneficial for stiff muscles, particularly for recent injuries and any sensation of bruising.

Ruta cream is more valuable for injuries to tendons and ligaments.

Tiger balm is an ancient Chinese recipe, available as an ointment. It contains stimulating and warming oils which help in chronic back pain and stiffness of the joints.

Homoeopathy

Homoeopathic medicines have a somewhat different action from herbs although many of the preparations are based on medicinal plants. Homoeopathic remedies are made by a special process of dilution in which only infinitesimal proportions of the original therapeutic plant or mineral are prepared. The healing benefit is, therefore, probably achieved at a less physical level which cannot yet be satisfactorily explained. Nevertheless, homoeopathic medicines have proved a valuable adjunct in the management of back pain. They are particularly useful in acute situations.

Each homoeopathic remedy can be obtained in various potencies — the degrees of dilution — which are signified by a number after the name. The higher the number, the greater the dilution and the more powerful the remedy. Some remedies are more effective at lower potencies given frequently and others at higher potency and less frequent dosage. Select from the following according to the indications. You may need different medicines at different stages of the condition.

Homoeopathic remedies for back pain

Remedy	Indications
Arnica 6 A few drops of Arnica tincture may be placed in the bath water.	Aching from over-exertion. Tender bruised sensation of muscles. Acute injuries and strains.
Aconitum 6	Sharp pain with sensitivity to the touch; numb, stiff, bruised pain between the shoulders. A remedy for acute conditions.
Antimonium tartaricum 12	Dragging sacral pain, violent lumbosacral pain. Feeling of weight on the coccyx.
Bryonia 6	Sensitive to the touch. Every move hurts.
Calcaria fluoricum 6	Weak tissues and slack ligaments.
Kalium carbonicum 6	Sharp cutting pains improved by motion. Intense neuralgic backache. Small of the back feels weak. Backache in pregnancy.
Ledum 6	Sharp stabbing pain
Pulsatilla 12	Shooting pain in the nape of the neck and between the shoulders. Pain in the sacrum after sitting.
Ruta 6	Pain after manipulation. Lumbago worse in the morning after rising. Inflammation of the ligaments. Backache improved by pressure and lying on the back.

Rhus tox. 6	Pain in the small of the back, aggravated by sitting and improved by lying on a hard surface. Stiffness, bruising, or burning sensation which improves with motion. Sensitivity to weather changes.
Silica 6	Weakness of tissues and ligaments.
Symphytum 12	Pain in the bones. Bones sensitive to the touch.

Dosage of homoeopathic medicines

Homoeopathic medicines are available from homoeopathic pharmacies and some chemists and health food stores in tablet form. In acute pain, use one tablet every one to two hours, reducing to every four hours with improvement. In chronic or less severe situations, use one tablet three or four times daily.

Homoeopathic tablets should be dissolved in the mouth and must not be administered within one hour of taking food or strong drinks, especially coffee, tea, and alcohol, or in close proximity to the use of toothpaste. All these items may negate the effect of the homoeopathic remedy.

Biochemic tissue salts

These are a series of the basic mineral compounds, prepared in low homoeopathic potency according to the principles established by Dr W.H. Schuessler. They are sometimes known as Schuessler Salts and may be obtained from health food stores and some chemists as cellules which dissolve easily in the mouth.

Biochemic remedies are taken in doses of four cellules every half to one hour for acute pain, and three to four times daily for longer-term treatment. They are also available as combinations of the most important remedies for specific conditions.

One or more of the following may be found to be of value

in the management of back pain.

Tissue salt	Indications
Calcium fluoride	Dragging pain in the low back. Strains.
Ferrum phosphate	Muscular pain, especially aggravated by movement.
Magnesium phosphate	Sharp pains. Muscles stiff.
Potassium phosphate	Pain aggravated by motion. Nervous sensitivity.
Sodium sulphate	Rheumatic pains aggravated by the damp and at night.

Coping with stress

It is no coincidence that the back gives trouble during periods of stress. If you are a sufferer from chronic back pain, just think back to the times when you had an acute episode. The chances are that when your neck got stuck or your lower back seized up there was a lot going on in your life: extra business pressures, an impending house move, or an unhappy phase in a relationship. That is when it gives way, and it is often at the most inconvenient time. It is one of the ways your body says 'Slow down!'

The interaction between our thoughts, emotions, and physical functions is constant and if we sometimes have a problem maintaining the balance between them, it is because of the 'fight or flight' mechanism with which we have all been provided as members of the animal kingdom.

Being the most highly evolved animals, we have developed ways of controlling these primitive impulses but in some respects this has been our problem. Unlike most other animals, we have developed the power to reason and rationalize, which means that we can also be unreasonable and irrational. It is through the nervous system, made for our protection, that these mental states create our physical pains.

Triggering the tension

The nervous reflexes which perpetuate the muscle spasms through the feedback mechanisms described in Chapter 2 are also triggered off by messages from above. Impulses travel down the spinal cord from the brain in response to its arousal for various reasons. The motor nerves which transmit instructions for action from the spinal cord to the muscles are of two main types. The alpha nerves help us to maintain coordination of our movements, preventing unnecessary contractions which may have been fired off mainly by the second, smaller type of fibres, the fusimotor nerves.

The fusimotor nerve cells in the spinal cord release a steady stream of impulses to the muscle spindles, inducing a state of partial contraction and readiness for action. They are part of primitive nerve pathways that are more active in animals in the wild, which need to be in a greater state of alertness. They are still quite lively in infants and young children, whose movements are less coordinated, but as we get older we learn to control them so that we can perform fine movements without the intrusion of unnecessary muscle contractions.

Although we have developed a good degree of control over the limbs, there is still a considerable amount of fusimotor activity to the muscles of the back and neck. This activity increases when we become anxious, tense, or frightened — our primitive instincts are preparing us to fight or run away. If you are in a perpetual state of over-arousal, always on edge, or undergoing constant crises, continual day-in, day-out firing of the fusimotor nerve cells will perpetuate stiffness and rigidity of the spine. No amount of osteopathy, chiropractic, and compresses will overcome this if the tension is persistently triggered by these unresolved conflicts.

When there are added short-term traumas the whole burden becomes too great for the back, especially if it is physically out of condition or poorly nourished. The adaptive processes are overwhelmed and you are forced to stop or, at least, slow down enough for your compensatory mechanisms to reestablish themselves.

Coping with the overload

We are well-equipped to cope with stress — in fact we need it to keep us alive and active. But we all go through periods in our lives when it becomes too great and the danger of 'going under' is greater. Whether or not we do depends on the coping strategies we have learned to utilize. Those who are worn down by over-commitment, work pressures, family demands, and being constantly 'on the go', will get by if they can pace themselves and use resources wisely to help them to cope better. The ability to cope, however, varies tremendously between individuals.

There are numerous ways you can buffer yourself against the ravages of stress and reduce your vulnerability to the precipitate attack when the pressure is on or the longer-term tension which perpetuates your stiffness is taking its toll.

* Understand your temperament.
* Counselling and psychotherapy to gain insight to personality.
* Physical discharge of aggressive tendencies or passive retreat by well-designed exercise.
* Reduction of arousal and physical tension by biofeedback, relaxation techniques, and meditation.
* Adequate sleep.
* Taking the 'hard edge' off your dominant negative emotions by the subtle approach of Bach flower remedies.

Posture and personality

The position which we adopt when standing or sitting is a reflection of a variety of aspects of our upbringing. Apart from the physical strengths and weaknesses of the joints, which determine the shape of the spinal curve, it reveals something about our attitude to the world — whether we feel bowed down by the burdens of responsibility (bent and round shouldered) or have a rigid unyielding attitude (stiff and straight).

Temperament and your back

To a certain extent, the way we cope with life's slings and arrows is determined by our constitution and personality. We all have predominating temperamental tendencies. They may be determined partly by our physical make-up and inherited susceptibilities, and partly by our up-bringing — whether we are taught to be over-dependent or excessively ambitious, for example. This is not to suggest that you can always blame your parents for your backache!

Although we cannot pigeonhole personality in a neat fashion, it is possible to give broad guidelines which may help you to understand how you may be contributing to your back problem with your attitudes and behaviour. Naturopath Peter M. Goldman N.D. has classified nine types of personality according to their behaviour and physical tendencies. Perhaps you will recognize aspects of yourself in one or more of these. If you do, you need not feel branded but you may be able to spot when these traits are beginning to get the upper hand. (NB: The gender used in these descriptions is of no significance; they may apply equally to both sexes.)

Go-getter

This type of person is competitive in both work and play. He has a gambling temperament and is inclined to overwork, pushing his body to extremes. This creates muscle tensions which may be resolved by rest and alternative stresses, such as exercise, which will discharge the aggressive tendencies.

Lymphatic type

This person tends to be lazy and indecisive. He lives with a sense of anxiety and feels that he is a victim of the postural problems to which he is prone. His back troubles are related to connective tissue sluggishness and may have a nutritional basis. There is also a low tolerance to sugars, fats, and milk in the diet. This type needs stimulation — exercise and tonic treatments to promote circulation and lymphatic drainage.

Hypermobile type

This person is structurally loose, hyperactive, and over-reacts to other people's personalities. There is an impulsive and emotional temperament with a tendency to dramatize problems. He is often accident prone and may be inclined to hysteria.

Indispensable type

The indispensable type feels he must work away incessantly and then feels sorry for himself when he gets over-tired. He is easily over-burdened with responsibility and his back problem is really other people's problems.

Schemer

Here is another gambling type, who feels capable of changing every situation and tries to manipulate others in doing so. He does not know his limits and becomes over-indulgent, even addictive. A lack of self-discipline goes with a tendency to hypermobility of the joints.

Perfectionist

This type is compulsively correct in actions and deeds. He is over-cautious and conservative and, because he is fearful of possible dangers, a tension is generated in the spine owing to the inability to let go and move naturally and freely. Excessive restraint leads to over-rigidity.

Martyr

The martyr absorbs and dramatizes the suffering of others. He may be Bohemian and disorganized in his habits, and this trend can be reflected in the rather poor muscle tone and lack of coordination in movements.

Sporting type

Another competitive personality who likes to win and to be in command. This person needs appreciation for his achievements. He needs to be encouraged to delegate, to relax, and to take regular breaks.

Independent type

This person becomes very concerned with the state of his own health and likes to take personal responsibility for it. He may, however, become frustrated by the lack of choice in taking action, and by not being able to do all he wishes about his health.

These are, of course, labels, and, as Peter Goldman says, few people will fall neatly into any one category. Many of us may be a composite of several types but where a clear pattern emerges it is possible to assist with relaxation, counselling, and the Bach flower remedies.

Spot your hang-up

Even if it is not always possible to clearly identify your nature, if you have a stubborn back, either stiff or unstable, it is worth reviewing the principal emotional states which may be providing you with some unnecessary ballast on your journey through life. These can range from fear, indecision, apathy, accident-proneness, and withdrawal from life, to feelings of over-responsibility, impatience, rigidity of outlook, and perpetual over-agitation and aggression.

As with faulty postural habits, recognition of dominant personality traits is a big step towards helping yourself to cope with them.

Relaxation and meditation

There are many forms of relaxation and you will need to find one to which you can relate and respond.

Techniques involving breathing and visualization (the use of imagery to induce physical changes in the body) are helpful for many people. These can be assisted by tapes on which the speakers may use a form of suggestion.

Some of these relaxation routines are based on the methods of L.E. Eeman, who used the principle of polarity in the body to establish normal energy flow and thereby induce relaxation. Eeman's system of relaxation has many similarities to the more recently developed and increasingly popular method of autogenic training.

Biofeedback
For those who find it difficult to release tension in muscles, biofeedback techniques may be helpful. In biofeedback a simple electrical apparatus is used to record changes in the skin resistance and to 'feed back' information about your state of relaxation. The information can be relayed by the machine audibly, with a bleep or buzz, or visibly, on a meter. The intensity of the audible signal, or the measurement of skin resistance on the dial, reduces as you learn to relax the muscles. Biofeedback is a good monitoring system for muscle tensions but for overall relaxation other systems, such as meditation and the Eeman relaxation routine, may be more beneficial generally.

Sleep

One of the consequences of over-arousal is a poor sleeping pattern — either difficulty in getting to sleep, light and restless sleep, or waking early. When this happens you get less of the deep phase IV sleep, during which most healing and regeneration takes place.

Relaxation techniques and tapes may help. A useful physical measure is to spray or sponge the feet and legs with cold water for two minutes before retiring, or if you wake in the night.

Exercise

The constant firing of the fusimotor nerves builds up a tension in the muscles of the back and neck which sometimes requires the discharge of physical activity. This may be particularly pronounced in the Go-getter and Perfectionist.

The exercise needs to be introduced gradually and, if possible, non-competitively. It should not become another stress or cause for anxiety.

Taking the edge off the temperament

The physical and mental inducements to relaxation can be backed up by softening the sharp edge of our temperament with the gentle nudge of plant power. Dr Edward Bach, a physician, discovered that the distilled essences of certain plants, when taken by mouth, or even rubbed on the skin, could exert a gentle influence on the mind. He devoted a major part of his working life to the discovery and development of the 38 plant species which have the properties of modifying such states as fear, impatience, feelings of overwork, irritability, and aggression.

The Bach flower remedies are available in stock bottles of liquid from which two drops of one or more preparations are placed in a dropper bottle, which is then topped up with spring water. Half a teaspoonful of brandy is added as a preservative. Just two drops of this mixture are then placed in any drink to be taken several times a day.

The Bach remedies seem to act at a very subtle level, in a similar way to homoeopathic medicines. There are a number of Bach flower remedies which may be of help to people with back problems. The following selection are plants whose indications include states of mind which can affect the back in one way or another.

Bach flower remedies

Bach flower	Indications
Agrimony	Insomnia, churning thoughts, restless at night.
Aspen	Fears of various things.
Beech	Intolerance, irritable with tension.
Elm	Overwhelmed by responsibility, though only temporarily.
Heather	Self-centred.
Hornbeam	Weariness of mind and body.
Impatiens	Irritable, impatient, tension.
Mimulus	Fear, stage fright, afraid to use the body (feels fragile).
Oak	Overworks.
Pine	Overworks, self-reproach.
Rock water	Taut, tightened-up person, rigidity of outlook.
Vervain	Lives on nerves, highly strung.
Water violet	Aloof, disdainful, leading to physical stiffness.

(Based on *The Dictionary of the Bach Flower Remedies* by T.W. Hyne-Jones, C.W. Daniel, 1976 and *The Twelve Healers and Other Remedies* by Edward Bach, C.W. Daniel, 1952.)

11. USE, MISUSE, AND ABUSE

Giving your back the best chance

As the mainstay of your body, the spinal column has an important influence on how you function mechanically and it is at the mercy of your postural habits. Using the spine efficiently in everyday activities, whether sitting at the desk, washing your hair, lying down, or lifting things, can contribute much to the prolongation of its active and effective life. Even the way you stand and walk has far-reaching effects on your health.

Postural habits

Habits of use are accumulated over many years, often imitating our parents, or other influential adults around us, in the postures we adopt. If their example is not a good one, a pattern of misuse can develop which may have far-reaching consequences for our health in later life.

There are many eccentric and intriguing variations on the normal human posture but they can be divided into two broad categories, the sloucher and the thruster (see Fig 29).

The *sloucher* adopts a stance in which most of the important joints of the body lie in front of the centre of gravity. The effect is for the knees to be under strain, the thigh muscles shorten, the pelvis tips forwards, the abdominal muscles sag, the chest sinks in, the breathing becomes more shallow, and

Fig 29 Poor postural habits can lead to numerous health problems

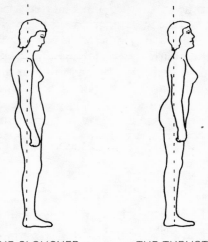

THE SLOUCHER   THE THRUSTER

the chin is pushed forwards and down. The consequence of this may be throat problems and chest disorders, because of the congestion in this area and the shallow breathing habit, the pendulous 'beer gut' drags down the abdominal organs and as the tone becomes weaker, constipation and uterine prolapses are more likely. Congestion in the pelvic region may also contribute to prostate troubles in males, and other, gynaecological, problems in females. The pressure on the veins in the base of the abdominal cavity interferes with their drainage, and varicose veins and haemorrhoids may develop. The weakened muscles also increase the likelihood of her-nias. The exaggerated curves of the spine itself impose extra stress in areas such as the neck and upper back and the lum-bar curve tends to be increased, with the muscles shortening. This makes arthritic wear in the joints much more likely.

The *thrusting* type tends to push the chin forward and up, so the neck muscles shorten. The bottom may be pushed back or the whole of the lumbar area may become flattened. The centre of gravity falls in front of the main joints, shoulders, hips, and knees, with alterations in the postural muscles. Some of the health problems arising from this posture may include headaches, dizziness, throat problems, chest disorders, breathing irregularities because of restricted diaphragm movement, hernia, and bladder problems.

When you see this catalogue of the consequences of postural abuse it will be obvious that it is worth making some effort to use the spine effectively. Education in posture should begin at an early age by instilling awareness of the body and its dynamics. Sports, games, and dancing, provided they are not too regimented and rigid in technique, help children to develop a sense of the postural muscles and to learn poise.

Walk tall

The main rules to observe when thinking about your posture are very simple but when you try to apply them they may feel strange and uncomfortable if you have become accustomed to faulty body use. Nevertheless try to observe these principles as you move about your daily activities.

* Walk tall.
* Imagine that you are being pulled upwards and forwards by a rope attached to the top of your head.
* The centre of gravity should fall through the ears, shoulders, hips, knees, and just in front of the ankles.
* Your weight should rest slightly on the balls of the feet.

Poised, alert, ready to move forward with confidence and comfort, you will draw the spine out to its natural open S-curve with the weight distributed more evenly through the joints and intervertebral discs.

The principles of conscious self-awareness and postural re-education are the basis of the Alexander technique which is explained more fully in Chapter 13.

Are you sitting sensibly?

One of the principal reasons for the epidemic of back pain in the late twentieth century is the large amount of time many

Fig 30 Sitting – try to give good support to lower back

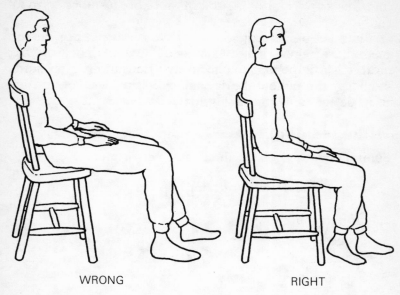

WRONG   RIGHT

people spend sitting, either through necessity or indolence. Whether you are sitting for work or leisure you can minimize the strain on vulnerable spinal joints by applying a few simple rules to the choice of furniture.

The worst fault of most seating has been to allow the vulnerable lumbar spine to sag into a gap between the backrest and the seat. This stretches the muscles and compresses the discs. It also restricts the breathing and crowds the abdominal organs. An added problem lies in the compression of the hip joint when it is at right angles to the trunk, as it most commonly is when sitting in normal chairs. As you lean forwards from this position the pressures are increased — for the sedentary worker this is going on throughout the day.

Dr A.C. Mandal, formerly Chief Surgeon at the Copenhagen Finsen Institute, has studied the ergonomics of the workplace for many years and his research indicates that the best position is to open the angle of the hips to about 135 degrees. This calls for a slight forward tilt of the seat and an adjustment of its height to enable the legs to be freer. In this position the spine tends to move into its more natural S-curve, the stomach area is relieved of compression and the diaphragm and rib cage are able to function more freely.

A number of chairs and stools have now been designed to meet these demands (see Chapter 12). When choosing your seating it is important to remember that your position needs to change throughout the day and a certain degree of flexibility in design is worth paying for.

Office seating

Some points to look for in an office chair are:

* Adjustable forward tilt for typing, writing, and table work, which returns to a more horizontal position for upright phone work and discussion.
* Adjustable back rest to support lumbar spine.
* Adjustable height for variable work surfaces.
* Swivel for easy access to side areas.
* Castors for mobility around the work station.

Leisure seating

Most people with chronic back pain view deep, soft settees and armchairs with alarm. A few minutes slumped in the enveloping softness will usually guarantee several hours of stiffness once you are able to clamber out.

You will be better off with a comfortable upright armchair — the carver chairs made for dining seats are usually satisfactory. Manufacturers of ergonomically designed seating generally have armchair models which are adaptable.

Driving

Until the last few years the design of car seats has not been considered an important selling point by motor manufacturers. Styling and streamlining seem to be more significant to the average motorist than comfort.

Motoring is becoming a little more agreeable with back pain but, with a few notable exceptions, most car seats still leave a lot to be desired. Like armchairs the biggest deficiency lies in the lack of adequate lumbar support. The best seats provide this with adjustable firmness and degree of curve. For those which don't, there are a selection of detachable back rests and lumbar cushions available.

Before setting off on a car journey take the time to adjust the car seat, particularly the angle of the back rest. This should be positioned to minimize the need to bend the head forwards. Once you are underway try to stop every couple of hours to walk around. Crowded abdominal organs, compressed discs, and sluggish leg veins will appreciate the change of position and movement.

Remember that car seats deteriorate. As they get softer the support gets less effective.

Beds

As we spend almost one third of our life in bed it is essential to get the maximum value from it. When we are reclining and sleeping the discs, free of compression, can take up more fluid and nourishment, which are gradually lost during the day.

Effective rest is a matter of time and money. Time is needed to choose and use the right bed, and money to invest in the best for your particular needs.

It is the mattress that matters; provided that you have a firm base you can choose the most comfortable one. Beds with slatted bases are ideal. If there is no suitable base the mattress on the floor is just as good. Japanese futons provide good firm support and are often provided with a base frame which allows the air to circulate beneath the mattress.

The important requirement is firm support for the whole length of your body with sufficient 'give' for the prominent parts to sink in. In other words, if you lie on your side, your spine should be almost straight, whilst your shoulder and hip sink in a little. The firmness, therefore, depends on weight and its distribution on your body and legs. The heavier you are, the firmer the mattress, particularly if you have a large frame. Large framed people have heavier limbs than those who are naturally small but who may have put on weight.

Having chosen your bed wisely — and only time will tell if you have — making the best use of that precious third-of-your-life time will depend upon the position you adopt when you lie in it. The best position for complete physical relaxation is flat on your back, but once you have been through a relaxation routine you can, if you are still conscious, turn over and sleep in your favourite position. For some people this may be huddled up in a ball on their side, for others an ungraceful sprawl on their front. If the latter position is adopted, keeping the limbs clear of your body prevents the pins and needles due to pressure.

As a general rule lie as flat as possible, with no more than one low pillow or a neck rest, if you can sleep on your back. The advantage of sleeping on your back is that no joints need be under pressure or strain and complete relaxation is possible, provided that the surface is of the right consistency.

Orthopaedic beds

These are specially designed beds with a firm base and mattress, which can be individually tailored for people who have chronic back disorders. They generally add reinforcement at levels where the weight distribution is likely to be greater. They are worth considering if you have persistent trouble and if you don't mind the extra expense.

As it is the time during which the body regenerates damaged or weakened cells and replenishes the energy dissipated during the day, relaxation and sleep are an important part of the back care programme. Get all you need at night and grab what you can during the day in the way of cat-naps and siestas.

Lifting and bending

The simple rules of standing and sitting can also be applied to most other movements in which you engage with work or play. Each activity needs to be done with forethought so that it is performed with the best mechanical advantage for the spinal column. This means keeping it as straight as possible so that pressure is spread evenly through all the discs.

The knees and hips have the flexibility and strength to do the main bending. When you bend forwards with the spine there is a concentration of pressure at the apex of the curve. This is all right occasionally for a healthy back, but, if it is a movement you perform often, the two or three discs in the region of the main curve will be repeatedly squeezed and may be worn thin. Arthritic changes may occur in the joints because of the extra friction and the spinal ligaments become stretched with the consequent stiffness of the muscles which endeavour to compensate for this.

Whether you are half bending over a wash basin, or right to the ground to plant bulbs, the effect is the same — it just focuses on different parts of the spine.

Stay straight to take the strain

When you are lifting and carrying the same stresses are exerted upon the spine, but they are increased by the need to counter-balance the weight you are lifting. The heavier it is,

WRONG   RIGHT

Fig 31 Lifting – holding the weight closer to the body with your back straight is more efficient and less strenuous

the more pressure there will be on the spine, and the more tense the muscles will have to be to support it. Staying as straight as possible will, of course, help the spinal joints to share the load more evenly. (See Fig 31.)

Squat when you can, but, if you have much to do at low level, kneeling reduces the strain on the hips and knees. Gardeners can use kneeling mats. For chronic back sufferers, raised flower beds are worth considering.

Raised beds for sleeping on are also easier when it comes to making them each day. Modern beds are lower than their predecessors, so it has to be down on the knees for them too, especially if you have to put the mattress on the floor!

The cantilever effect

Making use of the cantilever effect can improve the efficiency of your lifting and carrying. The mechanical principle of the cantilever is used in building some bridges. The arch is supported by placing the greater mass of the structure close to the supported end. This outweighs the maximum possible weight at the centre so the bridge remains stable.

When you lift anything heavy, the further away it is from your centre of gravity, the more pressure on the spine and its muscles. If you hold it close to you the distance from your centre of gravity reduces and the counterbalancing tension of spinal muscles and pressure on discs is proportionately reduced.

So, when lifting or carrying large packages, furniture, or children, try to keep them close to your body rather than carrying them at arm's length. To pick up a child, try to get your force through the bent arms and push upwards. Avoid twisting the spine with the feet fixed while lifting. Instead you should use the legs to turn your body.

If you have to lift out of awkward places, such as a car boot, try to brace yourself with one leg against the car and keep the load as close to your body as possible. When moving furniture it is generally easier to pull than to push. Try to stay upright when pushing and pulling, bending the hips and knees rather than the spine.

12. GADGETS

A consumer's guide

The phenomenon of back pain has, over the past hundred years or so, prompted some bizarre and complicated inventions for dealing with it. There is now a wide range of stools, chairs, and other devices on the market which you can use at home to help keep the back in good shape. Most are very simple in concept, and often steep in price, and whether or not they are a worthwhile investment only you can decide. This guide to some of the things available may help you.

Fig 32 Posture stool

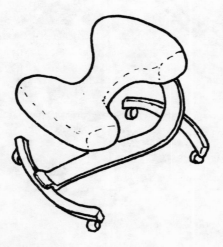

Stools and chairs

The evolution of the posture stool has passed the initial phase of austerity in sitting and moved to more considerations of comfort. The Balans series were the originators of the sloping seat with knee support and they have continued to lead the field, with developments in the design of leisure seating and more versatile office chairs.

Posture stools were the first in the new breed of special seating for back maintenance. These have a sloping seat with a support rest for the knees so that you sit with your feet tucked below you (Fig 32). This encourages you to adopt a healthier position for the spine, relieving pressure on the lumbar discs and the abdomen.

It is still possible to slouch on these stools and prolonged sitting gets a bit hard on the knees. The posture stool is

Fig 33 The Balans tripos – a work and leisure chair

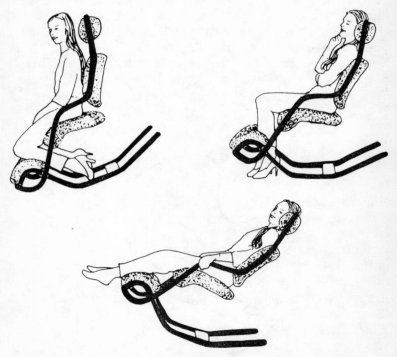

available with a rocker base for the various demands of desk or table work, or a fixed base with an adjustable height and angle. Castor-mounted models, with a swivel and a vertical hydraulic adjustment, are also available.

More elaborate use of the same principle is applied to the *Balans tripos*, a combined leisure and workchair, which can be used in the forward kneel position or as an armchair or recliner. (See Fig 33.)

At the top end of the market come office chairs of very sophisticated design. The *R H Activ Executive Chair* is a multi adjustable chair with a synchronized floating seat. The back height can be increased to include a neck rest; it is curved to cushion the shoulders. The lumbar support is adjustable and can be inflated to suit every back. Arm rests allow good working position in relation to the desk. The 'waterfall front' slopes to allow the thighs to drop when leaning forward. The seat height adjusts and the base can be fixed or free-floating so that it tilts as you lean forwards or sideways. The chair is mounted on free-gliding castors.

An alternative design, suitable for desk or drawing board work, is the *Ergoform Workseat Plus* which can be adjusted for height and angle. It allows you to work in a perched position or to lean backwards in a more conventional sitting position for lower desk work or typing. Variations of these designs are also made by *Labomatic* (which has a weight-activated hydraulic cylinder to change the angle of the seat and body positions as you move) and *Creda*.

These state of the art seats are all available at executive prices. If you do not spend your whole working day wheeling big deals you may find some simpler compromises worthy of consideration and accessible with your financial resources.

Putnam's Backrest is a simple, portable padded and shaped cushion, which can be placed in any chair or car seat to provide extra lumbar support. Alternatively, the *Putnam Wedge* is designed to be placed on the working seat to give the beneficial downward slope to the thighs, which gently rocks the pelvis forwards. It is tilted to just over ten degrees — ideal for desk or table work.

For travellers who have to endure train and plane seats, a specially shaped inflatable cushion provides convenient support. Just blow it up and place it in the small of your back, or higher up. An inflatable neck cushion is also available which embraces the neck like a life jacket so you can sleep in the sitting position without fear of waking with a nasty crick.

Spinal supports range from the *Backfriend*, a shaped moulded seat and backrest which can be placed in the car seat or a chair, to the *Schukra*, a more expensive lumbar support which can be adjusted to different pressures. Both these are portable and well-padded. Before buying a back rest make sure that it will fit in your car seat.

Backswing — an apparatus for graded traction
(Photograph courtesy of Health at Home Ltd)

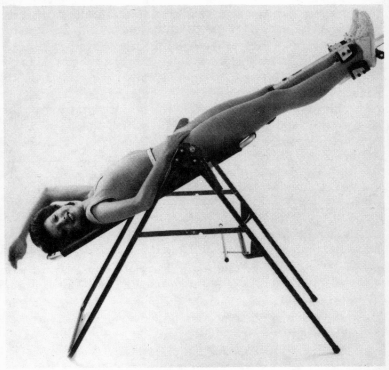

Resting and reclining

A good position for taking the weight off the spine when resting is essential. Various contoured recliners are available which tilt from semi-reclining to recumbent with legs raised. This gives good circulatory drainage to the extremities.

The principle of traction using gravity lies behind the design of the *Backswing*. This apparatus uses the weight of your body to provide a gentle, graded traction. With your feet on special rests you secure your ankles in padded clamps then lean back to the horizontal position. From there you can tilt yourself backwards to partial or full inversion. There is a gradual opening of the disc spaces while you remain in this position as gravity provides the traction. A home model is available which is suitable for body weights up to 14 stones (200lb/90kg) with a 7 foot (2m) ceiling height. It is wise to take professional advice before using this equipment.

Mattresses

Many mattresses use synthetic fibres nowadays and these do not provide the good insulation which improves sleep. A tufted wool or fleece under-blanket which covers the entire sleeping area of the bed can be placed between the bottom sheet and the mattress, and is held in place by elastic corner straps. This insulation maintains an even temperature in winter and summer, and sleep is said to have improved in trials carried out on people who experienced pain at night.

Pillows

Shaped neck pillows can be used for uncomfortable necks at night. The *Sommelier Pillow* incorporates the principles of the oriental neck roll and is made up of three sections: a low middle section, with two symmetrical and slightly deeper sides. The firmer sides are used to support your head while you are lying on your side, whilst the middle section supports the nape of the neck when you lie on your back. A flexible normal pillow which can be bunched up to meet your needs when lying in different positions may be equally serviceable.

Massagers

A good pair of hands are the best equipment for massage but some vibratory massagers can take the effort out of it. They also have the advantage of stimulating deeper tissues and promoting lymphatic drainage.

There are basically two types of domestic model. That with the bulb type hammer-action vibrating head is suitable for spot massage of small areas, but it is too lightweight to influence much more than the superficial tissues.

The models with a laterally vibrating plate (to which various spiked-rubber or bulbous attachments can be fitted) are slightly stronger and have a deeper effect, but require two hands to be used effectively. Such equipment is worthwhile only for regular use on stiff or sluggish muscles.

Some vibrators are available which use sound waves.

Vibratory cushions

An electrically heated cushion which is placed in an armchair supplements the warmth with a vibration — usually at a choice of two speeds — to give relief to stiff muscles. This is comforting for the more heavily built, well muscled person, but tends to be too disturbing for those of more slender build. The vibratory cushion is reputed to be of some value for the chronically stiff and arthritic backs but is a luxury at the price.

Fig 34 Spinal massage rollers

Ma Roller

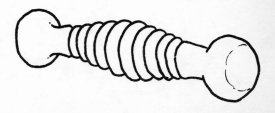

A cheaper, battery-operated vibratory cushion, without the heat, is also available.

Wooden rollers

A pleasant variation on normal massage is the use of polished wooden rollers. Specially shaped hardwoods are used and these impart a particularly pleasing sensation to the skin. Both the *Backdoctor* and the *Neural Easer* are devices with rollers attached to a long handle so that you can work them up and down the tender muscles on your back.

The *Ma Roller* is shaped to provide pressure to the muscles on either side of the spine when you place it on the floor and roll your back over it. You need to be fairly agile to do it, and the pressure of body weight can prove mildly agonizing over areas of muscle spasm! It is also reputed to stimulate the energy channels which lie on either side of the spine.

Pleasant though they are, most massage devices are quite superficial in their effect and are no substitute for proper care and professional attention.

13. GETTING PROFESSIONAL HELP

Where to go and what to expect

The care and advice of a practitioner is essential for successful management of all but the mildest forms of backache. It will be evident from the explanations of the causes of back pain that there are many situations in which a careful diagnosis will be necessary and specific treatment required. The self-help treatments described in this book are valuable first-aid measures, and essential adjuncts to the skills of your practitioner, but they can never be a substitute.

The situations in which you may need to seek professional help are listed on page 50. A good rule-of-thumb is to get a professional opinion for any discomfort which has persisted for more than three days. If any episode of back pain has incapacitated you, you should seek an opinion, even though you may now have recovered.

Choosing a practitioner

There are now a wide range of therapies available, many of which can contribute to the management of back disorders. This may make your choice a difficult one, but there can be no doubt that your first opinion should be from an osteopath or chiropractor. These professions have the diagnostic skills to determine the main cause of your discomfort, combined with a conservative approach to treatment which will not lead you to needless surgery, or other heroic procedures, without a careful consideration of the gentler options. They may also be able to save you endless days or weeks on your back in bed and countless pain-killers. Both osteopathy and chiropractic have an excellent record in getting people back to work after an episode of incapacitating back pain.

The spine is dependent upon many factors for its well-being. These range from postural habits to adequate nutritional and emotional nourishment, so there are a variety of professional skills you can draw on to help these. Some systems of treatment may be more appropriate than others at different stages of your disorder and you will be guided in what is best by your practitioner. A number of practitioners are qualified in skills other than their basic discipline. For example, some osteopaths also practise naturopathy or acupuncture, whilst others may have herbal or homoeopathic expertise.

Osteopathy and chiropractic

Both these forms of treatment have fundamentally the same objectives, so it will be convenient to consider them together.

Osteopathy was founded in 1874 by the American, Andrew Taylor Still, as a system of manual treatment to joints of the spine and other parts of the body. Chiropractic was founded about twenty years later by D.D. Palmer. Still's principle was that misalignments of spinal vertebrae interfere with the circulation to vital organs, thereby disturbing bodily functions, while Palmer and the chiropractors emphasized the nervous disturbance arising from such displacements (which they call subluxations).

In practice the difference between osteopathy and chiropractic was, and to some extent still is, one of technique. Osteopaths use a longer lever to make their adjustments and corrections of joint misalignments. Chiropractors use more direct and abrupt techniques, and tend to concentrate principally on the spinal column itself — indeed D.D. Palmer regarded the neck as the primary area of importance. Both osteopaths and chiropractors do, in fact, treat a wide range of disorders by working with the spine. Nevertheless, their greatest claim to fame has been as resolvers of back pain.

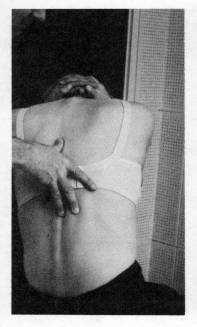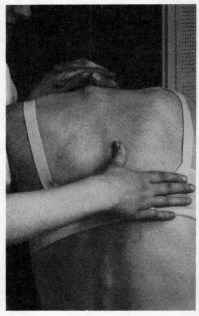

Osteopathic treatment of the upper back

What happens when you visit an osteopath or chiropractor?

If you consult an osteopath or chiropractor about your back pain, he or she will first take a case history to determine the nature of the discomfort, its duration, the sort of movements or other factors which aggravate or relieve it, and how it started. These all give clues as to which structure in the spine may be involved. The practitioner may also wish to enquire about your general health as this will have some bearing on your condition and its prospects for recovery.

You will be required to undress to the underclothes for an examination. First your posture in the standing position will be assessed and you may, if you are able, be asked to perform some simple movements such as bending sideways or bending the knees to tilt the pelvis.

Next you will be examined in the sitting position and the range of movement of the spinal joints may be checked by moving your head or trunk gently. Then, with you lying on your back, leg lengths may be assessed, and other spinal mobility tests may be carried out. The flexibility of the postural muscles will also be tested by raising and bending the legs and arms.

Some practitioners commence their examination with a spinal meter. This is an electrical device with a probe which is moved lightly down each side of the spine and this detects areas of heat and congestion which may signify joints under stress. These give a reading on the meter dial which indicates an increase in the skin resistance.

Finally, you may be asked to lie face downwards in a comfortable position. The practitioner can then feel the spinal bones and muscles carefully for possible abnormalities and displacements. Joints under stress will feel bruised and sensitive to gentle pressures applied by the fingers of the practitioner.

X-ray films are often required by both osteopaths and chiropractors. These provide useful information both with regard to the position of the joints and their pathological state. The films will need to be taken carefully, preferably in the standing position, so that the practitioner is then able to make assessments and measurements of the subtle changes of angle of the vertebrae. X-rays can also reveal arthritic changes, loss of disc space and other signs of degeneration, as well as any bone damage from injuries or evidence of tumours or other disease which might restrict the type of treatment that can be carried out. Osteopaths and chiropractors are particularly alert to the clinical signs which would suggest malignancy or other reasons for avoiding manipulation.

They may also require blood tests or other laboratory investigations.

Osteopathic and chiropractic treatment

The examination often becomes the treatment as the practitioner checks the range of joint movements and feels the tone of postural muscles. If the muscles are contracted, for example, gentle stretching and releasing movements may be performed, with your participation, there and then.

Techniques of treatment vary enormously between different osteopaths and chiropractors, but all will endeavour to restore a more normal alignment of the spinal joints. Chiropractors will concentrate on individual vertebral displacements, often basing their adjustment on the careful analysis of the X-ray films. Some osteopaths will prefer to manipulate individual joints or mobilize them gently before adjusting the muscle tone. Others will first attempt to balance the postural muscles and use soft tissue techniques, leaving any specific adjustment of bones until later, if this is still necessary — often it may not be.

The osteopathic adjustment is carried out by positioning the neck or back so that the joints above and below the one in need of attention are stabilized, and then making a gentle thrust to release the locking of the facet joints. This may result in a slight click, snap, or crunching sound as the facets are moved apart. The noise is believed to be due to the release of a vacuum which develops in the joint capsule when it is under pressure. There can be an effective adjustment without this sound, and, even where the vertebra does not appear to move, the vibrational force of the osteopathic or chiropractic thrust will often set in motion a process of release and eventual restoration of normal alignment.

Do not expect a lot of clicks and cracks — they are not a measure of the success of treatment. If vertebrae in key pivotal areas are in need of attention only one adjustment may be made at that visit. The spine must then be left for a few days to realign itself. This may be particularly applicable to adjustments of the atlas or axis, the eighth to tenth thoracic vertebrae, or the lower lumbar area.

The osteopathic and chiropractic adjustment is in no way a 'putting back' of displaced bones. Most bones do not move much when adjusted; they are merely released from a binding which restricts their normal range of movement. The adjustment allows the joint and its neighbours, which are nearly always involved, to regain some of their freedom to move in their normal range.

Osteopaths and chiropractors may also give you advice on hydrotherapy, diet, rest, and exercise, although they are unlikely to suggest the last of these in the early stages of acute back pain.

How long does it take to get better?

Although it is usual to get some immediate relief from your osteopathic or chiropractic treatment, do not expect your bad back to be cured after your first visit. Sometimes one or two vertebral adjustments can relieve the spinal restrictions and allow everything to settle down, but the 'hole-in-one', as the chiropractors call a single successful adjustment — usually of the atlas bone — is the exception rather than the rule. Even if the pain only started the same day, there may have been months, or even years, of postural abuse which laid their foundation, and the consequences of this may need a number of treatments to rectify if the risk of an early recurrence of the pain is to be overcome.

Acute pain often involves some inflammation and swelling around nerve roots. Even after an adjustment this will take some time to disperse and you may leave the surgery in almost as fragile a state as you entered it. Don't worry! If some gentle manipulation or muscle balancing has been possible, the body will start its process of recovery with the help of rest, fomentations, and other emergency measures (see Chapter 14).

Back pain of sudden onset may often be unsuitable for osteopathic or chiropractic treatment until you have rested and used the emergency measures for a few days. The effort involved in getting to and from the surgery may undo any good achieved by treatment. Some practitioners are occasionally able to visit patients who cannot move far, but only very gentle procedures will be possible until the inflammation and spasm have subsided. Nevertheless, these can be most helpful in getting healing under way.

When treatment is possible, most acute and chronic back pain will show signs of beneficial response within two or three visits — even if it wears off quite quickly. As treatment progresses the relief will last longer and the frequency of your visits may be reduced until you are self-sufficient. You will obviously be able to assist progress by carrying out some of the self-help measures in this book.

The cranial connection

For a long time a pretty hard-headed view prevailed
about the role of our skull in body movement. Because
the bones appear to the anatomists to be so firmly join-
ed together it was believed that the whole structure
was a solid case for the brain, perched on top of the
spine.

Then it was found that there is a rhythmical movement between the bones of the skull, which undulate
gently like the cogs of a clock as we breathe in and out.
Moreover, these rhythmical movements occur in harmony with those of the sacrum, at the base of the
spine. This subtle cranio-sacral motion helps to pump
cerebro-spinal fluid which bathes the brain and spinal
cord conveying nutrients to the nerve tissue.

Some experts regard the skull as part of the spinal
column. It has been suggested that restrictions in the
movements of the cranial bones may occur and these
may have repercussions on movements of the spine as
a whole. Causes of cranial lesions may range from birth
traumas, such as forceps delivery, to over-vigorous
dental extractions.

The cranial osteopath endeavours to restore normal
rhythmical motion of the skull bones by very gentle,
almost imperceptible manual techniques, using the
breathing of the patient to release restrictions.

Naturopathy

This is one of the major systems of complementary medicine
which gives attention to wider aspects of health. Naturopathic medicine uses treatment at a number of levels to encourage the restoration of the self-healing mechanisms. Most
naturopaths are also qualified osteopaths. They may give
more attention to nutritional factors and other aspects of life
style at the same time as treating the back.

What happens when you visit a naturopath?

Your initial consultation with a naturopath will be much the same as that with an osteopath and chiropractor, with a comprehensive case history and careful examination to determine the dynamics of your back problem. In long-standing disorders more attention may be paid to other aspects of your life style — nutritional, emotional, exercise, and postural habits — which could have a bearing on the problem.

Naturopaths make an assessment of the constitution and vital reserve before deciding on treatment and this may include inspection of the iris with a lens or a special apparatus. Iris diagnosis (iridology) is a valuable adjunct to other forms of assessment as the iris has zones which reveal information about various parts of the body with which they are reflexly connected. It is, for example, possible to observe signs of weakness at particular levels of the spine or indications that the efficiency of the stomach may be impaired which might have a bearing on the absorption of essential nutrients for spinal strength.

Naturopathic treatment

The initial treatment will, obviously, be directed at giving relief of pain or stiffness. Naturopaths make extensive use of the neuromuscular technique and other soft tissue procedures. The neuromuscular technique was developed by the pioneering U.K. naturopath, Stanley Lief, as a way of rectifying a wide variety of muscle spasms, adhesions, and joint problems.

The naturopath may also give advice on diet and the use of nutritional supplements as well as recommending hydrotherapy procedures. Naturopaths attach great importance to relaxation and can teach appropriate methods of reducing tension in conjunction with psychological counselling.

Acupuncture

Acupuncture, part of the system of traditional Chinese medicine which dates back several thousand years, has prov-

The mistletoe miracle

Mistletoe is a plant which has long been wrapped in mythology. Some of this is to do with its parasitic nature — it grows on the branches of deciduous trees, especially apple and black poplar.

In Germany, home of many legends surrounding the mistletoe, herbalists decided to try and apply the old 'doctrine of signatures' principle in which the physical features of a plant give a clue to its medicinal uses. If mistletoe is parasitic, they reasoned, perhaps it might have healing properties for 'parasitic' tissue in the body, such as fibrous degeneration or arthritic changes. Their theory turned out to be correct; the tradition has a physical foundation.

A special preparation of mistletoe which can be injected just beneath the skin overlying the joints will gradually stimulate the breakdown of fibrous tissue. It appears to reactivate the enzymes which restore the elastic fibres of the collagen.

The injections, used by a limited number of osteopaths and naturopaths, are given in a series of gradually increasing strengths over a period of five to six weeks and then at less frequent intervals for a few months. The results have been seemingly miraculous; many cases of osteoarthritis of the spine or degenerative disc disease have experienced relief of their aches and pains after years of suffering.

ed to be one of the most valuable forms of treatment for acute and chronic back pain. It consists of the insertion of fine needles into points on the surface of the body or the use of a dried herb, moxa, to warm them.

Although acupuncture has become famous as a method of pain control — having come to public attention partly through its use as an analgesic for patients who remain conscious throughout major surgery — it achieves other functional changes which, undoubtedly, account for its benefits.

What happens when you go to an acupuncturist?

At your initial consultation with an acupuncturist you may be asked a variety of questions on topics seemingly unrelated to your back pain, but be patient; they may, in fact, yield important information to the practitioner who is attempting to build up a picture of the total harmony of your body energy, the restoration of which is the objective of the treatment. The back disorder must be viewed in the context of your total health.

In Chinese physiology the functions of the muscles, ligaments, and bones are considered to be governed by the energies of the liver, spleen, and kidneys, and the acupuncturist may wish to seek indications of possible weaknesses and imbalances of these and other body functions as the basis of your chronic back disorder. Clues to these are given by observation of the colour of the skin, tissue tone, and, in particular, examination of the tongue and by feeling the pulse of both wrists. These are brief but essential assessments which the acupuncturist will need to make in order to decide upon the most appropriate way of treating the problem, even if the need is for more immediate pain-relieving measures.

When pain is acute the need for relief is of paramount importance and exploration of underlying causes is reserved for later. The practitioner will then concentrate on the aggravating and ameliorating factors and try to determine whether the pain is due to heat and congestion, calling for needles, or energy deficiency and lack of tone, calling mainly for moxibustion.

Acupuncture treatment

You may need to expose not only the affected areas of the back but also your extremities. The practitioner may then insert a number of fine, sterile, stainless steel needles a little way into the skin and muscles at points in the vicinity of the pain, and possibly on the arms and legs. These remote points lie on energy channels, or meridians, which either pass through the painful area or are connected with organs, such as the liver, spleen, and kidneys, which are closely involved with spinal tissues. Sometimes needles may be inserted at points along the distribution of referred pain, in the arm or leg, for example.

The insertion of the needles is a painless process, although a slight tingle, or impulse, may be felt as it reaches the energy channel ¼-inch (1-3 cm) deep. The needle may be left in for between ten and thirty minutes. Where more tone and strengthening of weakened tissues is required, the points may be heated with the burning herb, moxa. Small cones of the wool-like moxa are placed on the point, ignited, and allowed to glow until they feel hot, when they are removed. This will be repeated a number of times at each of several points bilaterally. An alternative method is to irradiate the point with a glowing stick of the moxa, held close to the skin, or the moxa may be allowed to burn on the handle of the needle in the point, which imparts a gentle heat to the energy channels and surrounding tissues.

The heated needles and moxa are particularly effective for osteoarthritis of the spine and for cases where pain arises

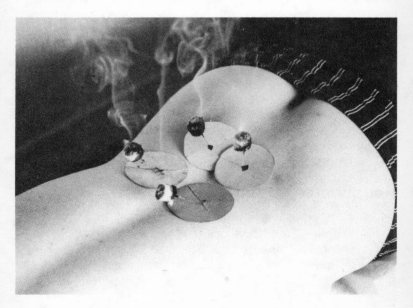

Acupuncture treatment with heated needles for chronic low back pain

from poor tone of the elastic tissues. Many cases of pain following laminectomy are helped by moxibustion, in conjunction with neuromuscular treatment.

Some practitioners may use other methods to treat the acupoints, such as *electroacupuncture* and *laser* therapy, though none of these modern developments have so far proved to be better than the traditional methods of needling and moxibustion. Another modern technique prompted by the acupuncture phenomenon and also using nerve reflex principles is *transcutaneous electrical nerve stimulation* (TENS). Electrical pads are placed on painful trigger points and given a low frequency stimulus with a battery-operated device. TENS is of value for cases of severe and unremitting pain, who can be given the equipment to use at home on a daily basis.

How does it work?

Modern research has demonstrated that the insertion of acupuncture needles induces the release of morphine-like hormones, the endorphins, which relieve pain, but these discoveries do not account for all the effects of acupuncture. The Chinese concepts of energy regulation still seem to be logical, and treatments are generally more effective when applied according to these traditional criteria.

For this reason above all, but also for proper standards of hygiene, you should, if contemplating acupuncture treatment, seek a fully qualified practitioner who has studied the philosophy and techniques of traditional acupuncture as well as its modern developments. Addresses of professional associations of qualified practitioners are given at the end of this book (page 184). Beware of practitioners, no matter what their other qualifications, who simply put a few needles in without really knowing why!

Physiotherapy

Physiotherapy is probably the most popular form of conventional help for back pain. It has long been a major tool in the National Health Service workshop and employs a wide variety of treatments. If you are referred to a hospital physiotherapist you may be given anything from electrotherapy to exercise, traction to manipulation, and, if you are lucky, you may even get some massage. Physiotherapists in private practice are more likely to have the time for hands-on work.

What happens at physiotherapy?

As your visit to a hospital physiotherapist, and to many in office practice, will usually be on the referral of your doctor or a specialist, it will not be necessary for a full case history to be taken. You will be asked to provide information about the circumstances in which your back is troublesome.

Examination will include mobility tests and assessment of passive joint and muscle movements — seeing how mobile they are when you are relaxed and not trying to move them yourself. One of the best guides to spinal well being is the ease with which you can perform everyday movements, such as putting on a jacket, putting on socks, doing up your shoes, and you may be asked to simulate these activities.

The physiotherapist may already have information based on X-rays which may have been done.

Physiotherapy treatment

In the hospital this may depend partly on the recommendation of the specialist, but the physiotherapist in private practice may have to decide independently. Physical therapy, massage, or joint manipulation — usually mobilizing and stretching, differing from the specific techniques of osteopathy and chiropractic — may be done in conjunction with an infra-red lamp to provide heat.

Other electrical treatments range from ultrasound to interferential and shortwave. These give a stimulus either by sound wave or mild electrical current to the deeper tissues to encourage drainage and dispersal of inflammatory waste products. Interferential treatment passively exercises the muscles by inducing contraction electrically. Exercises, often under water, are a major feature of physiotherapy treatment, the idea being to strengthen the back muscles and improve mobility. Pool work is particularly beneficial for people with arthritis and other handicaps.

Traction is often mechanical rather than by hand. Mechanical traction has one big disadvantage: the machine can't tell when to stop. If your neck or back is stretched there is a spacing of the joints at first but then a 'stretch reflex' sets in. The muscles go into spasm to prevent over-stretching of the joints. Traction in hospital may be necessary for only the most severe cases of ruptured or compressed disc which are causing intractable pain, but should only be intermittent and carefully controlled. Some physiotherapists use lasers, or TENS, and may also practise acupuncture.

Homoeopathy

Homoeopathy was established by the German physician, Samuel Hahnemann, in the eighteenth century. It is the use, in highly diluted form, of medicinal substances which in material dose might actually cause the symptoms being treated. The ingredients of Poison ivy (*Rhus tox.*), for example, would cause muscle constriction if given in a measurable quantity but in the classic homoeopathic remedy derived from it no molecules of the original plant can be detected and it is an effective remedy for the relief of muscular stiffness and rheumatism.

The remedies are generally based on plant and mineral substances. A number of low-potency homoeopathic remedies are valuable first-aid medicines for back troubles but for the deeper acting benefits you should visit a homoeopathic practitioner.

What happens when you visit a homoeopath?

The selection of the appropriate remedy from the many hundreds in the repertory requires a great deal of information, again seemingly irrelevant to your back problem. Most of the homoeopathic consultation may be spent just talking with you about your pains, their nature and intensity, how they, and you, react to weather change and movement, how you respond to other environmental changes, your temperament, preferences for hot or cold drinks and foods, and many other factors which will help the practitioner to identify the remedy which will best match your needs.

Homoeopathic treatment

Having selected one or two appropriate prescriptions you will be asked to take these, usually as tablets, with varying frequency, depending on how acute the trouble is. Chronic disorders may require medicines to be taken over many weeks with changes of the prescription according to your response. Homoeopathic medicine is a valuable adjunct to the management of acute back pain, often giving relief in a convenient way, which no other treatment can achieve. Its benefit in chronic back pain lies in helping the body to make subtle changes which will enable it to adapt to the mechanical weaknesses, which may also require more direct physical procedures.

Medical herbalism

The medical herbalist can offer valuable insights and approaches to chronic back disorders, particularly where they are associated with rheumatic tendencies and basically poor health.

The herbal practitioner can make more precise assessments of the herbs for you to take and their preparations. The herbal prescription may also be changed as your treatment progresses.

Herbal medicines may be prescribed as dried plants or roots with which to make an infusion, or as a mixture of liquid extracts to be taken as directed in warm water. The herbalist may also recommend poultices and liniments.

Alexander technique

This system of postural re-education was developed by an Australian actor, F. Matthias Alexander, who recognized that the vocal problems he was experiencing were related to the inefficient way in which he used his body. The methods he developed for correcting this are now taught by specialists who have undergone a rigorous training and personal experience of the Alexander technique.

Teachers of the Alexander technique make a careful assessment of your posture while you are moving, standing, sitting, and lying, and try to help you to become aware of its inadequacies and your faulty habit patterns. These may include slouching, lifting the chin, and tensing certain muscle groups unnecessarily. As you become conscious of these you will slowly be guided into more correct patterns of use with instructions on simple home exercises to encourage their development.

Alexander teachers vary in their approach: some will work with you sitting, others with you in the lying position. It will depend on what is considered best for you to develop the new awareness. The process of postural re-education can take anything from a few weeks to many months of regular sessions. It depends on the complexity of the habits which have to be untangled and redesigned.

Zero Balancing

This system of gentle body integration was evolved by Dr Fritz Frederick Smith, an American osteopath and acupuncturist, who sought a way of linking the structural principles of osteopathy with the energetic concepts of acupuncture.

The principle that energy moves in spirals, rather than straight lines, through the bones and around the joints in the body is the basis for the treatment in which gentle curved tractions or pressures are applied to the neck, back, and other joints. When this is done there is a general change of energy movement in the body which is indicated by signs the practitioner can observe.

The effect is one of structural release, which affects the whole body, but has great benefits for the spine where particular areas do not seem to 'let go' satisfactorily. Patients gain a sense of freeing and loosening of restricted areas after a treatment, while being spared the more vigorous techniques of most other manual therapies.

Zero Balancing is practised by some osteopaths, acupuncturists, and massage therapists. Although more profound in its effects, it is akin to the muscle energy techniques used by some osteopaths.

Conventional medicine and surgery

Although, for many people with back pain, these are frequently a first professional option, I have deliberately placed them last because, in spite of a high degree of technical skill in the diagnosis and management of back troubles, neither offers much in the way of personal responsibility and promotion of the self-healing processes.

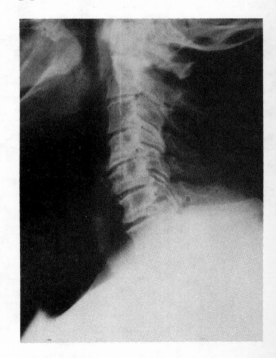

X-Ray showing side view of the neck. There is considerable osteoarthritic degeneration of the joints and narrowing of the disc spaces between the vertebrae. The patient regained freedom from pain after a series of osteopathic treatments.

Medical diagnosis

The sophisticated technology of modern medicine now provides information about the most intricate aspects of spinal and joint conditions, some of it of considerable value, and some rather irrelevant to the way your back may be actually feeling. X-rays, for example, may show loss of disc space and osteoarthritic degeneration but cannot explain why, after obviously having been like that for years, you suddenly start getting pain in the spine. Observations and intimate bio-chemical details of particular parts are of little use unless they are considered in relation to the workings of the whole system. X-rays only register the state of the bones, and many spinal disorders are more likely to be the consequence of soft tissue disturbances of one sort or another.

In cases where the intervertebral disc is suspect, a myelogram may be carried out. In this, a radio-opaque dye is injected into the spinal canal and then observed on X-ray to look for any indentation which may be caused by a protru-sion of the disc. Where the disc protrudes backwards into the spinal canal it may cause pressure on the cord or on nerve roots. The myelogram, however, can only indicate protru-sions into the canal, not in other directions. The dye remains in the spinal canal for some years and sometimes causes headaches.

The CAT scan (computerized axial tomography) gives the most complete picture of the state of both bones and soft tissues and is completely harmless to the patient. It is also ex-pensive and, therefore, reserved for the most difficult cases.

Medical treatment

Conventional treatment for back pain tends to be conser-vative (bed rest and pain-killers) or radical (surgery), with a few stages between, such as physiotherapy or injections. The choice seems to depend upon which specialist department of the hospital you end up in — the rheumatology clinic or the orthopaedic department. There does not yet appear to be a truly integrated approach to back problems in many hospitals.

Pain clinics tend to concentrate on pain control only, using various procedures ranging from drugs to TENS, without any programme of rehabilitation.

Injections may include steroids, for their anti-inflammatory effects; enzymes, such as chymopapain which 'digests' pro-truding disc fragments; or sclerosing agents, which are sup-posed to strengthen the elastic tissues.

Surgery, only after careful investigation to determine that it is really necessary, may be an effective solution where all else has failed. It is essential if there is severe disc protrusion (moderate protrusion can be reduced gradually by osteopathic treatment), or damaged bone or disc fragments causing pressure or irritation on nerve roots. The surgeon usually has to cut a window in the lamina (hence the term laminectomy) of the lumbar vertebra, to gain access to the nerve roots and protruding disc and relieve the pressure. Such procedures have quite a good response in 70 per cent of cases but orthopaedic surgeons are the first to admit that their approach must be a last resort. The cases with poor response may be attributed to various indirect factors, such as osteoarthritic degeneration, muscle wasting after surgery, and osteopathic misalignments at other levels of the spine such as the thoracic area.

Preventing osteoporosis – HRT or HNP?

Osteoporosis, a progressive loss of calcium and phosphorus from the bones, is said to affect one in four women after the menopause. It increases the fragility of the bones, causes back pain, and, if the vertebral bodies are weakened, a stoop or 'dowager's hump' may develop.

Oestrogen, the female sex hormone, which diminishes after the menopause, helps to prevent calcium moving out of the bones. A much vaunted preventative measure is to offset the natural reduction of oestrogen with a synthetically prepared form — hormone replacement therapy (HRT). Popular though this is, many naturopaths and doctors do not believe that the benefits justify the potential risks — known side-effects in a significant percentage of HRT users are cancer of the breast and cervix — particularly as safer preventative possibilities lie in lifestyle improvements and a healthy nutritional programme (HNP).

It is not just calcium in the diet which is important; a wide range of minerals, including magnesium, phosphorus, and vitamins, such as C and E, are also essential to support the body's natural process of change through the menopause.

The HNP consists of a diet of wholegrains, pulses, fresh vegetables, fruit, and dairy produce, with suitable supplements (see below) backed up by regular exercise to impress upon your bones the need to retain their calcium. One study has shown that thirty minutes walking a day can increase calcium reserves by as much as 2.6 per cent.

Osteoporosis prevention programme

Dolomite (calcium and magnesium) — 2 tablets 3 times daily.

Vitamin C (as bioflavonoids) — equivalent to one to two grams per day.

Vitamin E 100IU — 2 capsules 3 times daily.

A special German herbal preparation, based on the plant *Agnus castus*, is prescribed by some naturopaths and medical herbalists for its property of normalizing natural hormone balance during the menopause.

The integrated approach

The best prospects for recovery lie in an integrated approach in which neuromuscular treatment, nutrition, and hydrotherapy are used both before and after surgery, where this is necessary. If you are, or have been, a candidate for spinal surgery you may find many of the measures in this book of value to you.

Ask your surgeon exactly what he wishes to do and why, then get the opinion of an osteopath or chiropractor, just to be sure that there is not a more conservative approach to the problem.

Dealing with acute pain

A sudden attack of severe pain in the back or neck is a frightening experience. It can incapacitate you or, at the very least, make every move, or even a deep breath, agonizing, depending on which level of the spine is affected.

Fortunately, most attacks of back pain are not as severe as they may seem at first. Nevertheless, it helps to have a routine of management which you can put into action straight away. This will immediately minimize the pain, reduce the probability of further damage if the injury is severe, and promote the process of recovery.

Emergency measures

1. Rest

Immobilize the painful area in a position of relaxation. Lying flat reduces pressure on joints or compressed discs.

For *neck pain* place a small support under the nape of the neck.

For *back or leg pain* place a pillow under the knees. Experiment with a small pillow, or rolled hand towel, under the small of the back for a position which eases pain as you relax.

If *pain on one side* is severe lie on the affected side with the head well supported, to keep the spine straight, and a pillow supporting the upper leg.

2. Hydrotherapy

If you can, lie face downwards with a pillow under the abdomen. Get somebody to apply *alternating hot and cold formentations* (see page 61) to the affected areas for three minutes hot and one minute cold, repeated for twenty to thirty minutes (do not use ice unless there is very severe inflammation).

If there is no one to help you, it may be possible to apply hot and cold fomentations whilst sitting upright on a bathroom stool.

3. Homoeopathic medicines

For shock and bruising after sudden sprain or injury — *Arnica 6*, one tablet every one to two hours for five to ten doses.

For acute burning pain — *Aconite 6*, one tablet every two hours, reducing to four times daily with improvement.

For sharp, stabbing or lancinating pain (e.g. sciatica) — *Ledum 12*, one tablet every two hours reducing with improvement.

Very sore and sensitive to the touch — *Bryonia 6*, one tablet every two hours reducing to four times daily with improvement.

Turn to page 131 for more homoeopathic remedies.

4. Herbal medicine

For acute back pain with very sensitive tissues massage lightly with Olbas oil.

When less sensitive to touch and pressure apply a poultice or liniment of pepper and ginger (see page 128).

5. Massage

Gentle kneading above and below the area of sensitivity, i.e. work around the middle of the back for low back pain, and the shoulders for neck pain.

Gentle work on stiff muscles at the site of pain, if it doesn't aggravate the inflammation,

Turn to page 90 for more details on massage.

How to lift a person painlessly

One of the most agonizing experiences, when you have severe pain in the middle or lower back, is rising from the lying position. As soon as you attempt to sit up, the major muscles of the abdomen and back contract and squeeze the inflamed tissue and over-irritated nerves.

With the help of a friend it is possible to sit up with a minimum of effort on your part and a minimum of strain for your helper, regardless of any difference in size and weight.

(These directions are written for the helper standing on the right side of the bed. They can be reversed if the patient needs to sit on the left.)

* Place your feet apart with the left foot close to the bed and the right foot a little further away.
* Bend your knees and keep your back straight then place your left hand and arm behind the patient's neck or shoulders; place your right arm beneath his knees which should be slightly bent.
* When the patient is ready, lift him in one smooth movement by bringing your left arm up and across to the right while your right arm swings his legs towards you over the side of the bed. As you swing from left to right the patient pivots on his bottom into the sitting position.
* The whole movement should be completed in one sweep as you describe an arc with your arms. Do not hesitate half way or the patient might need to brace his muscles. Ensure that he is securely seated before letting go.

6. Reflex zones

Use the foot zones for the relevant area of the spine (see page 98). Apply gentle massage to this area for up to five minutes at a time every one to two hours.

7. Diet

Eat lightly of fruit or raw foods (salads etc.) or follow the cleansing diet (see page 113). Do not consume any alcohol, coffee, or strong tea. Increase intake of vitamin C supplement (1–3g per day).

As pain eases

Do not be tempted to become ambitious with your activities. Pain may have diminished but the mechanical causes may be still very much the same. Seek professional advice, to ensure that all is well before venturing to full-scale normality.

Backspeak — A glossary

analgesic pain-relieving substance or procedure
ankylosis fusing of the joints owing to degenerative change
articular pertaining to the joints
cartilage a tough, hard type of connective tissue which lines the joints
cervical the part of the spine which forms the neck
collagen protein-based material which forms muscles, ligaments, and connective tissues
disc a fibrous plate between the bones of the spinal column
ergonomic study of the postural aspects of the work-place
facet joint small synovial joints between the vertebral arches
fascia fibrous membranes supporting and separating the muscles
hydrotherapy treatment involving the use of water
intervertebral between the vertebrae
laminectomy surgical removal of the lamina of a vertebra
lesion any tissue abnormality but in osteopathy and chiropractic a disorder of muscles or joints, usually a displacement
lumbar the part of the spine from the waist to the hips
lumbosacral the area of the low back where the spine meets the sacrum
neurological pertaining to the nervous system
orthopaedic pertaining to structural disorders of the body

pelvis the ring of bone formed by the hips and pubic bones

rehabilitation restoration of normal function

Scheuermann's disease a degenerative condition of the spinal joints affecting mainly teenage males

scoliosis a lateral curvature of the spine

sinew a tendon

spinal cord the extension of the brain protected by the spinal column

spondylitis degeneration of spinal joints with inflammation

subluxation a vertebral displacement

synergist a muscle, organ, or substance working in cooperation with another

synovial a fluid which lubricates the joints; thus, a synovial joint has an encasing capsule containing it

thoracic the part of the spine from the neck to the waist which includes the attachments for the ribs

Back resource — professional bodies and support groups

Professional associations in the UK

General Council and Register of Osteopaths
1-4 Suffolk Street, London SW1Y 4HG (01-839 2060)

British Chiropractic Association
5 First Avenue, Chelmsford, Essex CM1 1RX
(0245-358487)

General Council and Register of Naturopaths
Frazer House, 6 Netherhall Gardens, London NW3 5RR
(01-435 7828)

British Acupuncture Association and Register
34 Alderney Street, London SW1V 4EU (01-834 1010/3353)

International Register of Oriental Medicine
Green Hedges House, Green Hedges Avenue, East
Grinstead, Sussex RH19 1DZ (0342-28567)

Traditional Acupuncture Society
11 Grange Park, Stratford-upon-Avon, Warwickshire CV37
6XH (0798-298798)

Register of Traditional Chinese Medicine
7a Thorndean Street, London SW18 (01-947 1879)

Chartered Society of Physiotherapy
14 Bedford Row, London WC1R 4ED (01-242 1941)

Society of Homoeopaths
2 Artizan Road, Northampton NN1 4HU (0604 21400)

British Homoeopathic Association
27a Devonshire Street, London W1N 1RJ (01-935 2163)

National Institute of Medical Herbalists
148 Forest Road, Tunbridge Wells, Kent TN2 5EY (0892 30400)

Society of Teachers of the Alexander Technique
3b Albert Court, Kensington Gore, London SW7 (01-584 3834)

International Institute of Reflexology
28 Hollyfield Avenue, London N11 3BY (01-368 0865)

Support groups

National Back Pain Association
31-33 Park Road,
Teddington, Middlesex TW11 0AB (01-977 5474)

Arthritis and Rheumatism Council
Faraday House, 8-10 Charing Cross Road, London WC2H 0HN (01-405 8572)

Scoliosis Association
380-384 Harrow Road, London W9 (01-289 5652)

National Osteoporosis Society
P O Box 10, Barton Meade House, Radstock, Bath, Avon BA3 3YB (0761 32472)

Professional associations outside the UK

Outside the UK, you should be able to obtain addresses from the Yellow Pages, but here are some suggestions for the USA and Australia:

American Association of Naturopathic Physicians
900 Madison Street, Seattle, WA 98104 (206 328-7971)

Traditional Acupuncture Foundation
American City Building, Columbia, MD 21044

International Foundation for Homeopathy
2366 Eastlake East, No.301, Seattle, WA 98102 (206 324-8230)

Australian Natural Therapeutic Association
31 Victoria Street, Fitzroy, Melbourne

Australian Traditional Medicine Society
Rozelle, Victoria

Australian Homoeopathic Association
c/o 16a Edward Street, Gordon NSW 2027

National Herbalists Association of Australia
27 Leith Street, Cooparoo, Queensland 4151

APPENDIX 3

Readback — more books about the back

The Book of the Back Brian Inglis (Ebury Press)
Your Painful Neck and Back J.W. Fisk (Arrow Books)
Neck and Back Problems Jan de Vries (Mainstream
    Publishing Company)
Osteopathy Leon Chaitow (Thorsons)
Naturopathic Medicine Roger Newman Turner (Thorsons)
Chiropractic — A Patient's Guide M.B. Howitt-Wilson
    (Thorsons)
Homoeopathic Medicine Trevor Smith (Thorsons)
The Healing Power of Acupuncture Michael Nightingale
    (Javelin Books)
Your Complete Stress-Proofing Programme Leon Chaitow
    (Thorsons)
The Twelve Healers and Other Remedies Dr Edward Bach
    (C.W. Daniel)
Dictionary of the Bach Flower Remedies T.W. Hynne-
    Jones (C.W. Daniel)
Osteopathic Self-Treatment Leon Chaitow (Thorsons)
Yoga Self Taught Andre von Lysebeth (Allen and Unwin)
Oriental Methods of Mental and Physical Fitness Pierre
    Huard and Ming Wong (Funk & Wagnalls, New York)
Massage Therapy Richard Jackson (Thorsons)
Better Health with Foot Reflexology Dwight C. Byers (Ing-
    ham Publishing Inc)

Index